Wings for the Wounded Soul

Finding Emotional Wellness
in God's Radical Love

Eileen J. Austin

WINGS FOR THE WOUNDED SOUL
FINDING EMOTIONAL WELLNESS IN GOD'S RADICAL LOVE

iUniverse books may be ordered through booksellers or by contacting:

iUniverse
1663 Liberty Drive
Bloomington, IN 47403
www.iuniverse.com
844-349-9409

Because of the dynamic nature of the Internet, any web addresses or links contained in this book may have changed since publication and may no longer be valid. The views expressed in this work are solely those of the author and do not necessarily reflect the views of the publisher, and the publisher hereby disclaims any responsibility for them.

Any people depicted in stock imagery provided by Getty Images are models, and such images are being used for illustrative purposes only.
Certain stock imagery © Getty Images.

ISBN: 978-1-6632-2861-1 (sc)
ISBN: 978-1-6632-2862-8 (e)

Library of Congress Control Number: 2021919662

Print information available on the last page.

iUniverse rev. date: 10/05/2021

DEDICATION

To my older brother, Peter Haik Jacobson, my first wounded warrior
   To Junior and Myra Mahaia, whose lives inspired many
   To my mother, Irene Jacobson
   To my grandmother, Takouhy Mangerian
   To my husband Rick
   To my children Peter, Mahea, Grace, Joy, Nicole, Andy, Whitney
   To my grandchildren Kayden, Obed, and Kawena Grace.

This book would never have been written without the loving support, inspiration and endless editing by my husband Rick and daughter Joy.

Friends and loved ones, who painstakingly corrected, commented and made suggestions chapter by chapter; so the material would be accurate and readable. They include Andy & Whitney Austin, Peter and Mahea Austin, Kahil Doty, Darlene Kelly, Wayne Kurashige, Lyana and Christian Neccyba.

CONTENTS

ACKNOWLEDGEMENTS

The author would like to thank the many prayer warriors including: Rev. Ralph Johnson, Troy Griffin, Lita Stark, Diane Nadeau, Larry Bozeman, Father Hovnan, Dr.and Mrs. Mark Owings, Ken Santorello, my friends Rosemary and Rachel, the New Hope Town Circle Group; Peter and Mahea Austin, Jaelyse and Peter Reneses, Wayne Kurashige, Leda Peni, and numerous loving neighbors.

The several skilled doctors who kept me alive so I could finish this book, including: Dr. Jim Etheridge, Dr. Gus Surrano, Dr. Bloom, Dr. Tabesh, Dr. Eschahol and Dr. Do.

PSALM 23

The Lord is my shepherd; I shall not want.

He maketh me to lie down in green pastures:

He leadeth me beside the still waters

He restoreth my soul:

He leadeth me in the paths of righteous for his name sake.

Yea, though I walk through the valley of the shadow of death,

I will fear no evil: for thou art with me;

thy rod and thy staff they comfort me.

Thou preparest a table before me in the presence of mine enemies:

Thou anointest my head with oil;

my cup runneth over.

Surely goodness and mercy shall follow me all the days of my life:

and I shall dwell in the house of the Lord forever.

BIBLE ABBREVIATIONS
USED IN THIS BOOK

Berean--Berean Bible
CSB--Christian Standard Bible
ESV--English Standard Version Bible
KJV--King James Version Bible
MSG--The Message Bible
NAS--New American Standard Bible
NET--New English Translation Bible
NIV--New International Version Bible
NKJV--New King James Version Bible
NLT--New Living Translation Bible
WEB--World English Bible

INTRODUCTION

In this book, *Wings for the Wounded Soul,* you will receive tools and strategies to help you identify and navigate your way through the maze of wounded emotions caused by painful past memories. These tools can help to maintain appropriate attitudes, thoughts and behavior even when knee jerk reactions to life's trials attempt to derail you. Inspirational stories, Bible scriptures, helpful information as well as probing questions are designed to help you dig deep, confront potential problems prayerfully, and then if you choose to, thoughtfully implement practical solutions to emotional healing. This book also identifies warning signs that tell you, it's time to reach out, text a friend or contact a professional, because this particular issue is too cumbersome, difficult or life threatening to handle alone. Each chapter also provides you with step by step instructions and bite size topics that help engage you so your true identity in Christ is revealed so you can renew your mind with action goals to help implement solutions. As the radical love nature of God is revealed, we remain secure in knowing we are God's treasures and are valued as His children, because He sees all of us through the lens of His precious son, Jesus Christ, and His sacrifice on the cross.

Out of the Belly of the Whale, my last book, chronicled my faith journey with God as I discovered and shared with the readers what the Bible had to say about physical healing. I hoped that by sharing my difficulties during kidney failure, dialysis, and finally the joy and freedom of receiving a kidney transplant from my older sister, Leilani Doty, would encourage readers to pursue healing regardless of how life threatening their diagnosis was.

With the completion of that book, I sighed in relief because my task was finished. Then God began to crystalize a new question in my mind. What role did emotions play as an obstacle to physical healing? When someone yields their emotions to God and allows their soul to be renewed, would that assist in the manifestation of physical healing? Obviously numerous physical healing are more complicated than that but it is still intriguing to imagine that some unseen emotional wounds inflicted by an abusive family member, spouse, teacher, boss etc. could be as debilitating as seen physical problems. For the person with spiritual awareness, a wounded emotion might also provide an access point for the enemy into their soul and keep them from embracing and fulfilling their God given destiny.

My prayer for you is that God will use the chapters in this book to remove any blinders and peel back layers of sin that have kept you from embarking on the spiritual journey of emotional healing. Don't be like Adam and Eve. Stop blaming others for what has happened to you and deal with the problem instead of 'kicking the dog' in frustration and running around in circles like a person caught in a revolving door! That is not to minimize or dismiss the role that others may have contributed to your difficult circumstances, but decide to move forward towards a positive lifestyle with God's help. Other steps to emotional healing include professing and acknowledging sin through confession, declaration, expressing contrite forgiveness from the heart and then renouncing and forsaking the sin and the old worn out path of negative thinking. This quality decision, with the Lord's help, will help launch you forward with a positive way of thinking and doing life. Finally, be patient with yourself when you mess up and trip. Start the process again knowing there must be ongoing active profession and pursuit, even if you feel at times that you are only crawling forward, remember at least you are heading in the right direction and be thankful for that. This is the divine pattern of walking in freedom and choosing a lifestyle of faith that includes healthy emotions.

A few years ago I noticed a distinct change in my vision when driving in the early morning hours or at night. Shimmering light haloes seemed to surround all the traffic lights. Anyone familiar with vision loss knows the frustration of having to stop reading because of eye strain or the harrowing fear of not being able to see clearly at night. No amount of squinting in front of the TV seemed to help clear up my vision. I tried everything from making one of my fists into a spy glass to look through, to putting on two pairs of glasses at the same time. My brain was working hard to fuse two different pictures into one. It was time to make an appointment with my optometrist, Dr. Wipfli, for new glasses; however, I was not prepared for the diagnosis he gave me. The culprit was an aggressive cataract forming on the lens of my eye. The solution he suggested seemed risky. I didn't want anyone messing with my vision unless absolutely necessary. Stunned by the news I asked him, how quickly I needed to act and what the vision in the left eye actually was. He did not reply but instead held up the eye chart and pointed to the big fat E at the top. No wonder driving was becoming so difficult!

Unlike this author, Dr. Wipfli was confident that with laser surgery, removal of the cataract and new lens implant plus correcting my refraction, my eyes would be seeing 20/20 in no time. But could I trust him? I asked him how many of these surgeries, he had done successfully and he said, he had stopped counting at 50,000. After much prayer and speaking with family and close friends I was encouraged to move forward. Scheduling the cataract procedure I thought about the obvious spiritual application. When things are not clear do you keep stumbling along in your life, hoping it will somehow get better or do you attempt to resolve the issue? If it requires an expert to help you, are you willing to swallow your pride, humble yourself and get the help you need and listen to people who have proven themselves trustworthy?

The surgery went exactly according to plan and within thirty minutes after surgery, I could see my hand perfectly. When my husband drove me home that afternoon, I marveled at the neighborhood pond where the sunshine sparkled like diamonds across the water, replicating my soaring emotions. The miracle of seeing everything I had been missing for so long included a delicate dragon fly with effervescent wings sitting on a lily pad. I couldn't stop praising God for his creation, my miracle eye and the doctor's expertise I had trusted.

My daughter Grace used to belong to a gym that financially supported a military veterans group called the *Wounded Warrior Project*. This nonprofit organization stated mission is to honor and empower wounded warriors while raising awareness and enlisting public aid for the needs of severely injured service men and woman of the United States Armed Forces. The greatest casualty according to them "is to be forgotten."

As I contemplated where to begin writing, the idea of a support group for wounded warriors intrigued me and kept returning to my mind. Could it be that some Christians are wounded warriors too? In church they bow their heads and humbly embrace God's mercy and forgiveness and experience emotional euphoria and a momentary victory lap at the altar? But when they return to their seats, will an experience alone translate into a changed life when courage and fortitude are required? What happens when trials and long standing character weaknesses persist causing them to return to their friends in the world?

A movie I watched sums up what I am attempting to address in this book. The main star, a female, kept a pocket size compact in her purse and the mirror was cracked. Every time she opened the compact to adjust her makeup, a friend noticed the fragmented mirror, so he asked why she used something that kept her from seeing her reflection properly. She replied that the broken mirror reminded her of how wounded she was.

Beloved, God doesn't want you living like that young lady with a broken reflection. He needs someone who is fearsome enough to partner with Him, confront the fractured past and press forward because He has lavished His love upon you. He wants you to seize this fabulous adventure called life. Like the method called Kitsugi where a broken dish is repaired with lacquer mixed with gold dust, our heavenly Father is in the business of repairing wounded souls, making all things beautiful by giving you beauty for ashes. Your biggest job is to allow the Divine Physician to remove the cataracts that have been keeping your soul from seeing how beautiful you are because that is how God sees you. Now, are you ready to start your journey with God back to healthy emotions, and embrace your amazing God given destiny?

> But unto you that fear my name shall the son of righteousness arise with healing in His wings. Malachi 4:2. (KJV)

CHAPTER ONE

New Beginnings

"Angels We Have Heard on High" was playing on the hospital intercom as the older brother marched the little brother down the ward and pointed to a plastic chair.

"Sit there till I come back."

Squirming in the chair, the disheveled six year old boy in mismatched clothes watched his brother disappear as he carefully pushed his dirty blond hair out of his eyes. He was clutching a gift crudely wrapped in old newspaper held together with plenty of scotch tape. Inside was a painted wooden stir stick that he had picked up on his last visit to the local hardware store. Gaudy crayoned pictures of yellow and blue Christmas balls decorated a tipsy green Christmas tree with a couple of red bells thrown in for good measure. Since it might be the last Christmas with dad, the boy decided to go all out and get him a present even though he didn't expect the kindness to be reciprocated. A nurse, in a white uniform, marched up to the boy and kindly offered an outstretched dark hand.

"Would you like to walk down the corridor and visit with Santa?"

This presented a small conflict. Receiving a present would be nice, but he had been told not to move. With a heave in his small chest, he decided to get into the long line filled with excited children.

When his turn came, the little boy climbed onto the big man's lap and Santa asked, "What would you like for Christmas little boy?"

The boy answered honestly, "Nothing for myself, but I got a question for ya."

The man in red tugged on his white beard and leaned closer, "OK, what is it?"

"Mister, do you know what God is like?"

Suddenly Santa flushed and looked a little surprised, certain this wasn't mentioned anywhere in his job description.

"Well, Dad is in room 701, and my big brother says he isn't going to be around for long. So I'm hoping God isn't like my dad because if he is, then Dad may be in big trouble!"

A lot of us are like that little boy asking the question of what God is like. We secretly hope he isn't like some of the abusive authority figures we have had to deal with in the past. If He is, all of us, like the little boy in the story pointed out, are in big trouble. Although we may be disillusioned, deep within the recesses of our heart we are hopeful that He is at the very least benevolent. Fortunately, truth seekers are in for a wonderful surprise because the loving nature of God through Christ Jesus has been revealed in scripture. So keep on reading!

Genesis: A Good God

As new believers crack open the Bible for the first time, we are introduced to God, the Spirit-Being, who is infinite, unchanging and loving. As we become acquainted with this merciful, benevolent and generous giver of all life, He seems too good to be true. Genesis, located as the first book in the Old Testament, is appropriately translated the Book of Origins because all things began with God. It is difficult to wrap our mind around this Holy God whose relationship with creation is on display as He demonstrates power, creativity and majesty in the expanse of the heavens, sky, earth and water. He fashioned a perfect universe and collaborated with His son while Holy Spirit brooded and awaited further instructions over the vast expanse. A massive star, the sun, brilliantly lit the world by day, while a reflective moon with a million dazzling stars crowded the black sky by night. Finally, in the great cosmos of planets, a perfect green and blue sphere, earth, was selected to be the home address for His children.

Billowy white clouds floated across an azure blue sky whose horizon was kissed by a turquoise ocean. Rainbow colored fish of every description and size as well as other sea creatures swam in an ocean teeming with life, playing in an underwater landscape's whose secret beauty would remain a mystery for centuries. Gorgeous trees hung heavy with ripened fruit of every color, description and size. They provided nourishment for the creatures large and small that roamed their emerald planet. Finally the piece de resistance was a small piece of land watered by mist and framed by four rivers. In this perfect garden paradise called Eden, God gently placed the pinnacle of creation, His two children Adam and Eve. Their job description was to take dominion, enjoy, explore and care for the garden and then fellowship and share their adventures with Creator, Father God.

Eating from the Wrong Tree

God spoke the world into existence, but he got his hands dirty as He fashioned the first family with his own two hands. Although their lives were perfect like all good parents, a warning was given about a danger that lurked in their midst. God had commanded Adam, "You are free to eat from any tree in the garden; but you must not eat from the tree of the knowledge of good and evil, for when you eat of it you will surely die." Genesis 2:16, 17. (NIV)

Looking back, we see there were numerous ways that Adam could have handled the situation of the forbidden fruit differently. Crystal clear instructions were given by God that this tree was off limits. Caretaker Adam should have kept a better eye on his wife by steering her away from the tree or at least trying to intervene and stop the conversation that she was having with the snake. However Adam was either beguiled or perversely curious about the fruit as they meandered around the tree of temptation day after day. Instead Adam should have sent that talking snake packing or pretended to look at his watch, pick a couple of bananas and head back with Eve to their rendezvous point with Father God. After all, the snake wasn't peeling fruit slices and dropping them into their mouths. With a million and one trees holding a billion and one pieces of fruit why did they choose the one that was forbidden? Scriptures gives us a couple of hints about why this fruit seemed so irresistible.

> Now the serpent was more crafty than any of the wild animals the Lord God had made. He said to the woman, "Did God really say, you must not eat from any tree in the garden?"

Eve spoke to the serpent, "We may eat fruit from the trees in the garden, but God did say, 'you must not eat fruit from the tree that is in the middle of the garden and you must not touch it or you will die.'

> "You will certainly not die," the serpent hissed to the woman, "For God knows that when you eat of it, your eyes will be opened and you will be like God knowing good and evil." Genesis 3:1-5. (NIV)

Looks can be deceiving as the old saying goes, and maybe the snake didn't appear to be threatening to them. Eve's seemingly harmless conversation with the creature ended with them giving their dominion over to the enemy. She wasn't satisfied to sin alone; she took a bite and then shared her experience with Adam. After all, it isn't fun to sin alone. Was this premeditation with Adam choosing not to be a goody two shoes? Perhaps ending up lonely in the garden without Eve was not an option for him, but his cavalier attitude had grave consequences. Perhaps God was exaggerating, they reasoned after all how bad can it be? They decided to be ruled by their flesh and independence rather than by truth and faith in what God had said. They knew what was right, but chose to do wrong. When thinking about why people choose to sin, it is important to remember that a seduction of some kind must be placed before them. In the case of Adam and Eve, they were told that they could be their own gods, knowing good and evil, and maybe they wouldn't have to answer to God any more. Sadly, they were about to learn the hard way that *God* wasn't the one who was doing the lying.

> When the woman saw that the fruit of the tree was good for food and pleasing to the eye, and also desirable for gaining wisdom, she took some and ate it and gave it also to her husband who was with her and he ate it also. Then the eyes of both of them were opened, and they realized that they were naked; so they sewed fig leaves together and made coverings for themselves. Genesis 3:6-7. (NIV)

As the story of mankind's beginning unfolds, we meet the first wounded warriors; Adam and Eve. We see the pair confronting life challenges with negative thought patterns that we immediately recognize. When God had created Adam and Eve, He clothed them in glorious innocence but now they had disobeyed God and responded by hiding, covering themselves with fig leaves and fault finding with each other. For the first time in their lives, they experienced a myriad of negative emotions including fear, shame, betrayal and suspicion. All of creation was now out of order with the serpent calling the shots instead of God and Adam and Eve.

> Then the man and his wife heard the sound of God walking in the garden in the cool of the day and they hid behind some trees in the garden. But the Lord God called to the man, "Where are you?" Genesis 3:8. (NIV)

Seduced by the words from a serpent and having consumed the

forbidden fruit, they tried to cover their tracks and nakedness by sewing fig leaves together. Sin was not in hearing the words of the snake, but in disregarding God's instructions and thus disobeying God. Now, rather than humble themselves before God, they tried to fix their own problem. It soon became apparent that they hadn't dropped dead, so perhaps they had already dodged the bullet. This is the thinking of everyone who partakes of sin. "I'm not dead yet. How bad can it be?" However sin was their new master and manifestations of sin emerged as they felt lost, vulnerable, fearful and naked for the very first time. Were they thinking clearly when their solutions included hiding from God in the bushes? He was the only one that held the solution to their dilemma so why did they choose to run? Knowing they weren't about to approach Him voluntarily, God decided to draw them out through a series of questions with the exchange revealing plenty of bad thinking and flimsy excuses.

> And He asked, "Who told that you were naked? Have you eaten from the tree that I commanded you not to eat from?" Genesis 3:11. (NIV)

Adam blamed the woman and Eve blamed the serpent. We don't know who the serpent blamed but you can be sure that he was looking for the nearest exit and scapegoat. To make matters worse Adam and Eve believed the unwanted guest in the garden was Creator God! When they lost their identity, they forgot who they were and what they were to possess. Unable to cope with overwhelming negative emotions, they hid their imperfections from the One who they believed revealed their flaws. In a moment of weakness they had changed teams, aligned with God's enemy and saw a Holy God through the jaded lenses of suspicious eyes. The couple was now in strife with God, one another and with creation.

If only they had responded differently but how could they? All along there was someone who continued to hang out with them in the garden. It was the serpent. He never left. Because once you invite Satan in, he is going to stick around and hang with you until you kick him out. He may even be the main stay in your life as long as your permit him. Only when sin leads you to sorrow and true repentance with an about face course and direction change, will that necessary reprieve occur. Imagine how different this story would have ended if Adam and Eve looked up with wide eyes honesty to God and said, "Oops, God, we are so sorry. We were wrong. Would you please forgive us?" But we do not read anywhere that they asked for forgiveness. Perhaps they didn't fully grasp the gravity of their sin and how many negative doors had just swung wide open through their simple act of disobedience. Being kicked out of paradise should have been a huge wake up call for them, but, tragically for the next generation, consequences are exponentially worse as one son murders the other. None of us truly understands the enormity of loss generated by sin because the ramifications are too numerous and its impact so far reaching, that we can't even imagine the destruction that is turned loose in our lives when we disobey God's instructions. In short, when communion with God is shattered then the authority and oversight we once had is broken as well. As my preacher friend Wally used to say, sin will take you farther than you want to go, cost more than you want to pay and keep you longer than you want to stay.

In the blink of an eye, creation had fallen, the two sinned and why, because they ate from the Tree of the Knowledge of Good and Evil rather than eating from the Tree of Life which would have given them the chance to be eternal. Now they had fallen into sin, trust was broken and God in His wisdom had to block access to that tree lest they become eternally lost. The cascading consequences of sin were now firmly planted in the garden resulting in paradise lost.

Since that time, the fruit of pride, sense and reason from the tree of the knowledge of good and evil have been in the driver's seat of humanity rather than humility, obedience and faith. Any time we try to determine, in our own wisdom and strength which part of this is good and which part

7

of this is evil, we have already lost the battle. God said, "Don't eat from any part of that tree." It was a test of belief and obedience to God's word and they failed. As we all know from our own experiences, there is never any true satisfaction from sin because it is never enough. Now that Sin had tainted the souls of our warriors and they were wounded and deceived, unable to think clearly, how were they going to put the proverbial genie back in the bottle? What would become of the two?

Perhaps you think that you would have done things differently, given the chance but the apostle Paul doesn't seem to think so. Paul indicates in the following passage that all of humanity struggle with simple faith and obedience to God's word. Remember when you have a decision to make, it will always include a choice between two trees, the Tree of Life which is to believe God and do what He says or the Tree of the Knowledge of Good and Evil which is to consult your own wisdom and lean to your own understanding and do what the enemy suggests. Bill Johnson of Bethel Church in Redding, CA says that any time you pass a test and go on to the next decision, God plants another tree so you can make another decision. Decide right and He rewards you, decide wrong and consequences follow. That is the essence of all tests. God can't reward people unless there is a choice. Remember any decision made without Christ at the center is demonically inspired.

The Deceiver: Stranger in the Garden

Eden breathed harmoniously with the life of God, but the serpent brought something foreign into the garden. Deception! It blinded Adam and Eve's eyes to truth and the enemy has been successfully using it down through the generations: sin wrapped in a personality and voice that contradicted, slandered and lied about what God said and what the consequences would be. Our natural senses, also referred to as the flesh, seem to crave and pull us downward toward sin. Maybe it's because of the dirt from which we were formed was cursed. Once Eve believed and agreed with the serpent, the fall quickly followed. Adam may have been in tacit in agreement (meaning just going along for the ride) or he may have been willfully disobedient. You can be sure that a lifetime of regrets followed. Would you have wanted to be in the house with Adam and Eve following their first failed test?

Keep this in mind: it wasn't a stray thought that entered Eve mind but a disobedient word from a stranger disguised as a friend whose sole purpose in life was to make her fall. Next time, a clear crystalized thought enters your mind slandering God's promises or a person close to you questions God's integrity. Stop in your tracks, remember Adam and Eve, and do not assume the idea comes from your own mind. It may have been planted there by an enemy. This couple did not sin alone, but got help from a serpent.

In my mind it is hard to read about this and not be frustrated as I imagine all that was lost and the painful consequences that followed. How can I sit in judgement of them knowing despite God's faithfulness to me in the past, I too balk at the next trial, vacillating between faith and doubt? Can I really trust His word this time? I know intellectually that God has always been there for me in the past and will always be there in the future, but my contrary emotions and my flesh are pressing their advantage and threatening to lead me astray by doubting what God has promised. Remember the cartoon picture of two little creatures sitting on the shoulders of a character in the cartoons; they are speaking into his ear, one sinister demon while the other is angelic light. Who will he listen to this time?

Adam and Eve were no longer innocent. In that single moment when creation fell, every evil thing imaginable entered in the world. Wickedness, wars, famine, murder, rape, pestilence, drought etc. etc. albeit in seed form, but they would quickly flower and produce evil fruit. To keep them from eating from the tree of life and being eternally cursed, Adam and Eve were driven from their beautiful garden paradise and into a world filled with withered plants, thorns, thistles and weeds. Innumerable broken dreams had been shattered, not only did they forfeit their innocence but passed down a death sentence to their heirs, us! If only the couple had stood their ground and answered the serpent with the truth of what God had said. Every test is either going to take you closer to God or pull you away from Him. The enemy has a fruit tree planted in your garden and God has one, now choose which one you will eat from. Fear or faith, truth or deception, faithfulness or disobedience, you cast the deciding vote.

Scripture Declarations

1. He restores my soul; He guides me in the paths of righteousness for His name's sake. Psalm 23:3. (NAS)

2. For I know the plans I have for you declares the Lord, plans that give me a future and a hope. Jeremiah 29:11. (NIV)

3. The effectual fervent prayer of the righteous avails much. James 5:16. (NIV)

4. For I am persuaded that neither death nor life, nor angels nor principalities, nor things present nor things to come, nor height nor depth nor any thing present nor things to come shall separate me from the love of God. Romans 8:38. (KJV)

Questions

1. List four characteristics of God that you have learned from reading this chapter.

2. This chapter talks about two trees, name them and explain what each of them represents?

3. Think about an area where the enemy has currently seduced you to sin, keeping you from your destiny. Based on what you read about Adam and Eve, what should your response be? (Hint: think about repentance.)

Action Goals

1. Now it's time to confess, renounce, and verbally forsake this problem area. Write down a game plan for what specific changes you would like.

2. Now prayerfully commit this area to God and ask for His help as you take the journey to full restoration.

Confession: Prayer of Commitment

Father God, as I take this spiritual journey to renew and heal my emotions from past pain. I ask You to please help me honestly confront my pain, sin and weakness from the trauma of my past even though it may involve tears and time to heal. Lord Jesus, I ask You to give me courage and with the help of your Holy Spirit, I plan to walk away from any unhealthy coping mechanisms and the toxins of my past life and embrace a life filled with joy, healthy emotions, my destiny and one with no regrets. Amen.

Chapter Notes

CHAPTER TWO

REGAINING PARADISE LOST

God told Adam and Eve that if they ate the forbidden fruit, they would die, so two very fearful individuals had to be coaxed out of the bushes so God could provide them with a better and more permanent covering. It must have been quite a shock, because up to this point they had no experience with death. Adam had personally named each of the animals. What conflicting emotions must have crossed his mind when he realized that one of his innocent animal's blood would have to be shed to cover their transgression, while the animal skin provided a covering for their naked bodies?

> It is the blood that makes atonement for the soul. Leviticus 17:11. (NKJV)

From that day on, under the Old Covenant, yearly sacrifices had to be made to cover sin. Israel continued to set aside a day of atonement, but this was a temporary measure because the blood of bulls and goats could never cleanse the conscience of mankind. God instructed the high priest to make a sacrifice on an altar to atone for his sin and for the sin of the people. Then he would take a scape goat laden with the people's sins and drive it into the wilderness. To insure the goat did not find its way back home, they would guide the goat to a cliff and drive it off. Apparently in the past, the goat would sometimes find its way back home, much to the horror of the community. Year after year, again and again, they came away from the Day of Atonement knowing that sin was just covered up, but never removed. Consequently the consciousness of sin was always lurking in the back of their minds!

> But those sacrifices are an annual reminder of sins, because it is impossible for the blood of bulls and goats to take away sins. Hebrews 10:4. (NIV)

God always had a plan to finally put an end to this endless cycle of sacrifices. In the New Covenant God sent His own perfect son, Jesus, as the ultimate sacrifice to pay for sin once and for all. Jesus shed His blood on the cross, so our consciences would be cleansed from dead works that we might finally stand in God's presence uncondemned. With our sins remitted or put away, we were finally justified and able to enter God's throne room boldly with our petitions as though we had never sinned. As sons or daughters of the Most High God, we must have a healthy respect for who He is, while being fully confident in what He has done for us through His son Jesus Christ.

> "The cross was where the old method of counting ended and the place where the new time began. The thing that stood between man and God was Adam's transgression. Jesus put that away." E. W. Kenyon

Communion: Do This in Remembrance of Me

When Jesus was baptized in the Jordan River, John said, "Look, the Lamb of God, who takes away the sins of the world." John 1:29. Three years later, on the night that Jesus was betrayed and before His crucifixion, He took the Passover unleavened bread and cup and instituted communion among His disciples as a way to identify with what He, Jesus Christ, was about to do on the cross. This was to affirm that He was indeed God's lamb of sacrifice. By taking His shed blood, their sin would be atoned for not by some animal but by His own perfect blood sacrifice. With the sins of the whole world atoned for, the broken relationship with the Father was now restored.

> For whenever you eat this bread and drink this cup, you proclaim the Lord's death until He comes. I Corinthians 11:26. (NIV)

Then we are asked by the Father to take this Good News to others, boldly declaring that all sin has been atoned for. The only missing ingredient is the individual who must personally accept this. When a person is born again, they become a follower of Jesus and part of a new family. The new family should support them in their new found faith by "showing them the ropes" just as young sailors were taught how to handle the ship by wiser and more experienced deck hands. This cannot be ignored, overstated, or overlooked because Christians were never meant to do life alone. Jesus said this to his disciples after His resurrection and before He was taken back to heaven.

> "All authority in heaven and on earth has been given to me. Therefore go and make disciples of all nations, baptizing them in the name of the Father, Son and Holy Spirit, and teaching them to obey everything I have commanded you. And surely I am with you always to the very end of the age." Matthew 28:18 -20. (NIV)

Jesus' words remind us that we must become familiar with the teachings in His book, the *Bible*. That means a daily and intentional commitment to learn the ways of God so a full restoration can occur in our lives from all the ravages of a sinful lifestyle. Think about it this way. Once a person enlists in the army of God, there is no turning back. There may be setbacks, but only deserters turn back. The life of the Christian must involve discipleship with the same type of commitment as an enlisted military person. Military training will impact every area of their life including when they get up, when they sleep, what they eat, who they train with and ultimately when and where they go. In short how they live their lives from that day on.

A drill sergeant calls the new recruits to work out with a group of peers, and as they progress, accountability to fellow comrades in arms increases. He knows they will need others to survive this journey. The focus becomes group success because those relationships may ultimately save their lives. Loners do not stay loners for long.

This means the church must rethink successful soul winning. It must be more than a church group bragging about how many people they led to the Lord in a single service. We are not slick vacuum cleaner salesman eager to make that one big sale. If someone can be talked into salvation then someone else can talk them out of it. Fledgling converts must understand that they are making an ongoing commitment to the church and believers, so they can reach maturity in Christ. We must go back to the New Testament model that Jesus set up for His disciples who gave oversight and accountability to new converts. They were brought into a family so that when their spiritual progress came to a standstill, they had someone to share their frustrations with, pray with, in short they had someone that was willing to go after and restore them to insure that they were not neglected and didn't become a Christian casualty. Jesus commanded His followers to make disciples of all nations, teaching them to obey everything He commanded them. This was not a one shot deal! No group on earth believes that an individual can become successful alone. Thankfully, the military does not believe this, churches should not believe this, families don't believe this and neither did Jesus. Community for the believer insures that they are equipped to complete their mission!

> Without council, plans fail, but with many advisers, they succeed. Prov. 15:22. (ESV)

A great example or picture of discipleship is the commitment that young parents make to selflessly nurture, love, and train a child until that child is finally ready to nurture a family of their own. When Rick and I took home our first baby boy Peter John a little more than 40 years ago, we didn't know what we were getting ourselves into, but we certainly oozed with ardor and zeal. Our love knew no bounds until reality struck. Those first few months of Peter's life were times of wonder as well as frustration that included lots of crying (from parents as well), feeding, rocking, numerous sleepless nights for two already exhausted parents and all those endless dirty diapers! We quickly realized that we needed a support system, so we enlisted the wisdom and aid of grandparents, aunts, uncles and friends in our church that would support our due diligence.

So it is with a new believer who has just found faith in Christ. They have been offered a fresh start and a new strategy to navigate life. Maybe alcohol or drugs, an immoral, alternate lifestyle or even personal family loss and tragedy left the individual without a moral compass or direction in life. Circumstances beyond their control brought them to the place where they recognized their need for a Savior and so they embraced Christ for the first time. They realized that alcohol, drugs and other vices provided an artificial support. Now they had the Holy Spirit to help them cope with challenges. Opportunities for a bright and hopeful future stretched endlessly before them. They had been forgiven by the blood that Jesus shed on Calvary for human transgression that allowed them to wipe the proverbial slate clean. Enthusiastically they volunteered for church activities every time the door was open and purchased a Bible that was probably big enough to choke a moose. They may have even learned some new phrases in a language I will refer to as *"Christianeze."* It short they had cleaned up.

As time passed, their enthusiasm waned with former struggles reemerging and persisting. Faith alone seemed insufficient to navigate the endless waves of hurdles as the new believer attempted to struggle forward. Without the necessary support system of a group who loved them unconditionally some of these newbies dropped off the church grid. They had abandoned church and maybe even returned to bad habits and old friendships that created the original problem. What went wrong with their new found faith? Why didn't they stick to it? Had they put in the sufficient effort to be successful? In short why had they become a Christian casualty? Like the support that came from the *Wounded Warrior Project*, they needed a group of people as committed to their progress and restoration as they were. They needed Holy Spirit's guidance, the church family for fellowship and Bible study for growth and nourishment. Relationships with seasoned saints were needed to help them light their way when the path seemed obscure. As our culture further disintegrates, it becomes even more critical that believers have the unwavering support, love and acceptance of their Christian family who are as 'committed to their progress' as they are.

Myra and Junior's Commitment

This next story is about a couple that decided to take God at his word and participate in the restoration that He offers each of us. Myra and Junior Mahiai made the decision to take a step in faith and found it made all the difference in their world.

It was Wednesday, about a week after Christmas. While checking my Post Office box, I noticed a card hidden and stuck against the wall of the box. Stretching my fingers all the way to the back I was able to retrieve the card. Curious, I looked on the back of the card to see who it was from. The return address indicated it was from Hawaii, a Myra and Clement Mahiai Jr. I had met Junior (Clement) Mahea's older brother and his wife Myra at my son Peter and Mahea's wedding in Hawaii a week and a half earlier. Even more chilling was the fact that Myra had died unexpectedly on a Wednesday, the day after Christmas. As I read the post mark, December 24, Christmas Eve, I called my son in Hawaii and began to carefully open the envelope. Myra had written a card and was literally speaking to me from the grave.

There is something eerie about receiving the card from someone who just passed away. I thought back to Saturday evening, December 22nd, the day after the wedding, recalling that our son Peter wanted the family to be together for one last meal before we all returned to the mainland. The Mexican restaurant down the street was close to the hotel plus the food was delicious. Grace, my daughter, and my nephew Kahil, had searched long and hard to find matching orange, University of Florida T-shirts, for a family picture. The best they could do was getting bright orange Hawaiian shirts for everyone from the local flea market. We smiled and put them on thinking about being 'that family' that wore matching Tee shirts for family vacations and reunions.

Dinner had grown to 20 people and Junior and Myra were one of the couples. It had been a busy weekend, the hour was late and I was tired, but my son Peter insisted that I talk with Myra who was experiencing kidney failure. I understood the discomforts and pain of kidney failure having experience it more than 14 years earlier. As everyone was hugging and saying goodbye, Myra stood alone off to the side alone. So, I decided to introduce myself to her. Soon she and I fell back from the crowd, walking slowly up the tiny hill towards the hotel, reminiscing about the beautiful wedding we had experienced the day earlier at the beach.

My husband, Rick, and I had walked our eldest son, Peter, down the flower strewn aisle to meet his beautiful bride Mahea accompanied by her parents Clem and Filomena. As they exchanged their wedding vows accompanied by the rhythmic sound of the waves, two enormous sea turtles, a good luck sign to Hawaiians, had crawled up obligingly on black volcanic rocks. A fitting background song *Somewhere Over the Rainbow* was sung by the famous Hawaiian performer, Iz Kamakawiwo'ole. Myra and I agreed that with the sun setting, a rainbow colored sunset had made the wedding seem magical.

As I shared my story, I became energized and seemed to wake up. Myra was breathing hard and coughed from time to time, but she seemed intent on hearing more about what I had to say as we headed up the hill towards the hotel. For a wedding gift, our daughter Grace had given the couple two days for a honeymoon at the same resort where our family was staying. Then Peter asked all of us if we wanted to go up to see their hotel room. This seemed strange to me, since my son and his bride Mahea were on their honeymoon but what mother can say no to her eldest son's special request especially when we had traveled so far to see him. The hotel staff made sure that Peter and Mahea wedding suite was amazing and had secured a corner room with huge glass sliding doors opening to a balcony that overlooked the ocean, now black. Looking out at the twinkling stars with waves pounding against the shore I thought about three wise star gazers who had traveled far to bring gifts to the tiny baby Jesus so many centuries earlier about this time of year. As the night wore on, various family members including myself shared personal testimonies of God's goodness along with sections from my book on healing called *Out of the Belly of the Whale* to Myra and Junior. We encouraged Myra to pray and ask God to personally assist her with her healing journey. The couple shared with us that they were Catholic but didn't attend church every week. My husband Rick assured them that receiving Jesus as their personal savior did not conflict with their Catholic beliefs, but would rather enhance their faith in God.

Peter and Kahil reminded Myra and Junior that praying didn't have to be fancy. Simple words from a humble heart were always sufficient when praying to their Heavenly Father. We reminded them of how much they were dearly loved by God, Myra and Junior didn't seem tired, but wanted to hear more and asked many questions which we answered to the best of our ability. We all had lumps in our throats when Junior added that when Pete and Mahea had publically exchanged their vows the evening before, he had taken Myra's hand and recommitted to himself to his bride of sixteen years and softly uttered the words *in sickness and in health for richer or for poorer until death do us part.* Kasy, one of Mahea's bridesmaids, leaned on her elbows and listened quietly on one end of the giant queen bed while my youngest son Andrew kept watch at the opposite end. In the peaceful atmosphere Kayden, Mahea's son, quietly listened and began to doze.

I opened my book and read the sinner's prayer to Junior and Myra and reminded them that making a verbal commitment of faith, asking God for forgiveness of sins and declaring their decision to follow Christ before witnesses was like the vows that Mahea and Peter had repeated to each other the evening before. Even though they didn't understand everything about faith, they both agreed to pray. Boldly taking the next step they were ready to approach God, Myra and Junior nodded their heads, held hands and recited the sinner's prayer from my book.

When Myra and Junior prayed *"The Sinner's Prayer,"* they began their personal relationship with God and His son Jesus Christ. By accepting the Lord and His sacrifice on the cross, they now had access to the precious Holy Spirit and all the promises mentioned in the Bible including healing. We told them this was the beginning of their healing miracle and the most exciting journey of a lifetime. To seal their new found commitment to the Lord, they wrote in their names along with the date in the book I had given them. We ended the evening by anointing Myra with oil and praying for God to help them navigate through the ordeal of sickness. Kahil and I were impressed that God was saying that Junior was very strong. Junior decided to pray over his new brother in law Peter and when he did he said he felt something like wonderful energy welling up inside of him. We told him that was the Holy Spirit putting His affirmation on the prayer. As quickly as this precious evening started it was now over but Junior and

Myra would never be the same because they knew that someone greater was now living inside of them and would be with them no matter what. None of us knew how quickly all of this would take on a unique meaning. Just after Christmas I received a phone call from Peter to tell me that Myra had passed away. What a relief to know that she was in heaven.

Now more than ten days later I was staring down at the card from Myra and Junior. As I opened the Christmas card, three wise men appeared and gazed up at a brilliant star. Tears began to well up as I read these words to my son.

To the Austin Ohana (this word means family in Hawaiian)

> May the Spirit of Christmas bring you Peace, the gladness of Christmas give you hope, (and) the warmth of Christmas grant you love,

Then in Myra's own hand she added the following words

> Mahalo Eileen and Rick for your prayers,
>
> I am currently reading your, Excerpts from Out of the Belly of the Whale. It was a great pleasure to have met you that night. Junior and I have so much to be thankful for. We will begin a new journey spiritually, thanks to you and your family.
>
> Love and aloha always, Junior and Myra Mahiai (Mahealani's brother and sister in law)

The card in my hand was something very, very special. In my mind, I recalled the songs at the wedding that Mahea had chosen. Myra with great excitement about the preciousness of their new decision had decided to write a Christmas Eve note to a family she barely knew and then mailed it. She never knew the powerful meaning this simple act would take on. The couple who had shared wedding wows with a couple as the song

21

"Somewhere Over the Rainbow" played had ended the experience with a song by Celine Dion called "The Prayer."

Could any of us take credit for the amazing and miraculous turn of events or was it just some bizarre coincidence? It was as if each player had been given very specific instructions and as they yielded their will an incredible evening happened. Grace yielded by giving the couple a chance to honey moon at the resort. My husband and I yielded to my son's fervent request to talk with Myra. Andy yielded when Kahil awoke him up and said we have to do something important. Finally Myra and Junior yielded to God when they responded to the invitation to receive Jesus as their personal Lord and Savior. An experience with God can be compared to a baby's birth. I believe that God by His Holy Spirit carefully orchestrated and prepared this spiritual birthing event for Myra and Junior.

How about you? Are you ready to take the leap of faith as it is sometimes called? No matter how many mistakes you have made or how unworthy you feel, remember this. God has already taken care of those mistakes or sins as the Bible calls them through the blood sacrifice of His son, Jesus Christ. By accepting Jesus as God's substitute as payment for *your* sins, **you can be forgiven**. This may appear to be overly simplistic, but I assure you it is not.

According to I John 2:12 and Romans 3:25, God put upon Jesus the wrath for our sins so that we don't have to bear the responsibility of them. A fancy word for this is called Justification. After your sin problem has been taken care of, you then can ask Jesus to come into your heart and become your Savior.

Scriptures:

1. Without the shedding of blood, there is no forgiveness. Hebrews 9:22.

2. For God so loved the world that He gave His one and only begotten Son Jesus, that whosoever would believe in him should not perish buy have eternal life. Whoever believes in Him is not condemned, but whoever does not believe in Him stands condemned already because he has not believed in the name of God's one and only Son. John 3:16 - 18.

3. If you declare with your mouth that Jesus is Lord, and believe in your heart, that God raised Him from the dead, you shall be saved" Romans 10:9.

Questions

1. What are the differences in the sacrifices made in the Old Testament as compared with the new?

2. What have you learned about communion that you did not understand before reading the chapter?

3. What is an example of what discipleship should look like in the church?

Action Goals

1. You are now going to be given the same opportunity, as Myra and Junior. Would you take the opportunity to receive Jesus as your personal Savior? If you have decided to make this decision, read the paragraph below under Declaration/Pray this and sign your name:

2. If you have not taken communion with the understanding you have gleaned by reading the chapter, you may want to do so now but only after you have received the Lord as your personal savior.

Declaration / Pray this:

Thank you, Lord Jesus, for coming and dying on a cross to redeem sinners. I believe that you exist and that I am a sinner. I ask You, Lord Jesus, to forgive me and please come into my heart and my life. I believe that you died on a cross for me and now accept and acknowledge you as my personal Savior and Lord. I ask to be filled with your Holy Spirit that I may live for you while I am on this earth, and then be with you in heaven after I die. Amen!

If you have just made a declaration and prayed then sign your name and place a date in the space below indicating that you have just ask Jesus Christ to come into your heart

Name _____ Date _____

Chapter Notes

CHAPTER THREE

SUCCESSFUL CHRISTIAN LIVING: TWO BAPTISMS

It was apparent that God had gone out of His way to kiss the marriage of Mahea and Peter by granting the greatest miracle of all. Mahea's brother, Junior and his wife Myra, had received salvation as a result of what they heard and who they had experienced. Introductions are important. For example, when Pastor Alex introduced the couple as Mr. and Mrs. Austin for the first time, everyone clapped. All of the seasoned married couples who were present knew that the young couple would experience a lot of bumps along the way, but the affirmation, blessing and support of love ones was appreciated. So it is with the novice Christian. Accepting Jesus as Savior is just the beginning of a wonderful adventure.

Baptism in Water for Repentance from Sin

Before Jesus began his earthly ministry, he was baptized in the Jordan River by his cousin John the Baptist. Although Jesus was sinless, He submitted to baptism or immersion in water representing repentance from sin *as* our example and for our benefit. After Jesus emerged from the water, the Spirit of God in the form of a dove rested upon Him. The Holy Spirit settled upon Jesus to empower, anoint and give Him the authority necessary for His upcoming ministry. According to Unger's

Bible dictionary, this act of baptism indicated His public submission or consecration as a priest.

> Jesus replied, "Let it be so now; it is proper to do this to
> fulfill all righteousness." Then John consented. As soon as
> Jesus was baptized, he went up out of the water. At that
> moment heaven was opened and He saw the Spirit of God
> descend like a dove, lighting on Him. And a voice from
> heaven said, "This is my Son, whom I love; with Him I
> am well pleased." Matthew 3:15 - 17. (NIV)

In Genesis 6, God shares an object lesson about the first world-wide cleansing event that occurred when the earth was baptized by flood waters. Prior to the event God expressed His concerns to His servant, Noah, and revealed His extreme remedy to cleanse the moral filth. Most of us remember the story from childhood: Noah building a great overstuffed arc that included a tiger, lion and perhaps a tall giraffe threatening to sink the awkward little craft. In reality the boat was the size of a football field, an architectural wonder that contained three decks and a design unique enough to allow the boat to float and bob on top of the flood waters. The back story on why the event occurred is important because it offers to us a unique foundational truth about our Creator that all of us would be wise to pause and ponder. God keeps an eye on His creation and will judge wicked mankind accordingly. Thoughts, emotions and actions of mankind are held up to His ever watchful scrutiny especially when they get out of hand. The unspoken lesson is if He did it once, then He can do it again. God's eyes saw man's wickedness and God's emotions felt grief and his heart experienced pain at the perverted man made mess.

> During Noah's time the Lord saw how great man's
> wickedness on the earth had become, and that every
> inclination of the thoughts of his heart was evil. The Lord

was grieved that he had made man on the earth, and His heart was filled with pain. So the Lord said, "I will wipe mankind, who I have created, from the face of the earth man and animals, and creatures that move along the ground and the birds of the air, for I am grieved that I have made them." But Noah found favor with the Lord. Genesis 6:5-8. (NIV)

New Testament Converts are Baptized

Just as the earth in Noah's time emerged from the flood cleansed and fresh to begin again so it is that individuals emerge from the cleansing waters of baptism. In the New Testament, baptism is the subsequent event for anyone who has been born again as a way to identify with their Savior Jesus Christ. Jesus commanded that his disciples be baptized to identify with Him by symbolically going into the watery (grave) and then rising out of the water (the resurrection) to experience newness of life. God commanded Christians to be baptized as an outward demonstration of an inward commitment to die to ourselves and be raised to live as obedient followers of Jesus Christ.

> Having been buried with Him (Jesus Christ) in baptism, and raised with Him through your faith in the power of God who raised Him from the dead. Colossians 2:12. (NIV)

Peter and the New Testament disciples practiced baptizing converts to symbolize union with Christ in His death, burial and resurrection from the dead.

> Then Peter said to them, "Repent and be baptized every one of you in the name of Jesus Christ for the remission

of sins and ye shall receive the gift of the Holy Spirit."
Acts: 2:38. (KJV)

Baptism of the Holy Spirit for Power and Authority

After Jesus' baptism in water, He was baptized with the Holy Spirit so His teachings were now accompanied by demonstrations of power that included miraculous signs, wonders and healing including deliverance from demons. Jesus demonstrated His authority and power, from the Father God, over all the works of the devil. There is an old saying, actions speak louder than words. The same should be happening to His disciples. That means you and me!

> "But if I drive out demons by the Spirit of God, then the kingdom has come upon you." Matthew 12:28. (Berean)

Evangelist Reinhard Bonke had this to say about the importance of the Holy Spirit, "It is not so important to think of the Holy Spirit in me. Rather we must ask, am I in the Holy Spirit? You can have a bucket of the ocean or you can be in the ocean, in one case you have the ocean but in the latter case the ocean has you." The Holy Spirit must be given free reign, so He may rid us of all the darkest places within the human soul that do not reflect His will or His ways or His thinking.

Any person that lives a compromised life will block out the work of the Holy Spirit in that unregenerated area, and will not reflect Christ in that area of their life. If God does not fully inhabit us, then we cannot fully function in the authority and power of the Holy Spirit. This may explain why some people's prayers appear to go unanswered in a specific area or seem ineffective in their Christian walk. They are saved, but not fully yielded. It may be necessary to go deeper into the word and prayer in order to meet the precondition of prayer. Of course, God is sovereign and can do whatever He likes. Oftentimes in scripture God's promises say if you will do thus and so, then I God can do thus and so. Sometimes by the decisions we make we actually prohibit the work of the Holy Spirit from operating in an area of our lives.

Francis Frangipane tells the humorous story of trying to use the included instruction manual to assemble his child's present on Christmas Eve. He quips that the finished product should have been a bike but unfortunately it looked more like a gyroscope with several left over pieces. Because he did not consult the manual sufficiently during the assembly process something was created that did not resemble the picture on the box. Sound familiar? If your image doesn't match up with Jesus or if you are not overcoming in a situation, consider prayerfully asking guidance from the Holy Spirit to find out where you went wrong in the process. Then ask the Lord to help get you back on course. In short, keep seeking His righteousness.

"But seek first the kingdom of God and His righteousness and all these things will be added unto you". Matthew 6:33. (Berean)

Pursuing Passion

The way we overcome the world, the enemy, and sin is to be fully yielded to the Lord. This will defeat any enemy within and give us the victory over any nagging bad habits and strongholds that keep us from fulfilling God's plan for our lives. It is God's super - on - our - natural that gives us supernatural ability. One must choose to pick up their cross daily, die to self and follow closely in the Lord's footsteps until receiving the desired results in all areas. Michelangelo once said "Every block of stone has a statue inside it, and it is the task of the sculptor to discover it." This is what God wants to do with us: chisel our stony hearts until only Jesus remains. Remember the cross of Christ and that there is power in His name and in His blood.

> Therefore, since we are surrounded by such a great cloud of witnesses, let us throw off everything that hinders us including any sin that so easily besets (entangles) us, and let us run with perseverance the race marked out for us. Fixing our eyes on Jesus, the author and perfecter (finisher) of our faith, who for the joy set before him endured the cross, scorned its shame, and sat down at the right hand of majesty on high. Hebrews 12:1. (NIV)

Jesus' miracles and healing deliverance were God's calling cards that represented the manifested kingdom of God on the earth. For this reason, the disciples never wanted Jesus to leave earth. They walked, talked and experienced Jesus' love, miracles and wisdom firsthand. But walking with Jesus did not prevent their shortcomings and humanity from surfacing regularly. As wonderful as those three years were, Jesus had to remind them that He had come for something greater. In the Old Testament, innocent animals like doves, lambs and bulls were sacrificed yearly at the temple, but they were an incomplete sacrifice for sin. They could cover sin for the year, but were unable to cleanse the conscience of man.

Jesus came to earth to die and pay the sacrificial price for sinful humanity once and for all with his own blood. When He ascended into heaven, He placed His sinless blood upon the Heavenly Holy of Holies. Only then was mankind's sin finally and completely atoned for.

> Day after day every priest stands and performs his religious duties; again and again and offers the same sacrifices, which can never take away sins. But when this priest (Jesus) had offered for all time one sacrifice for sins, he sat down at the right hand of God. Since that time, he waits for his enemies to be made his footstool. Hebrews. 10: 11-13. (NIV)

The Apostle Peter: A Paradigm Shift

The Apostle Peter's entire life was transformed by Jesus. Renamed Peter or Rock in John 1:42, he met Jesus through his younger brother, Andrew. One day the brothers were casting nets into the Sea of Galilee. After fishing all night they had caught nothing. Jesus got into their boat saying, "Put out into the deep water, and let down your nets." The next thing they knew, there were so many fish that Peter's nets were breaking. Simon Peter was ashamed knowing he was undeserving of such a miracle. Undaunted by this, Jesus said, "Come ye after Me, and I will make you fishers of men." Peter and Andrew witnessed numerous miracles after that.

> Simon Peter answered, "Master we have worked hard all night and haven't caught anything. But because you say so, I will let down my net." The next thing Peter knew, they caught such a large number of fish that their nets began to break. He fell at the feet of Jesus and said, "Go away: I am a sinful man," but Jesus said, "Don't be afraid, from now on your will catch men." Luke 5:5-9. (NIV)

Jesus had demonstrated his authority over the natural elements when he fed five thousand men, woman and children by multiplying five loaves and two fishes. As evening approached Jesus sent the exhausted disciples in a boat across the water while he remained and prayed. When the disciples were a considerable distance from the shore a storm came up with gale force winds, buffeting and tossed huge waves across the bow of the craft. Terrified and exhausted by their toiling, the disciples knew they couldn't keep the boat from sinking. With the storm at its worst, suddenly at the midnight hour, Jesus came walking on the water like a ghost. Peter cried out, "Lord, if that is really you then bid me to come." Jesus said, "Come." Immediately Peter stepped out of the safety of the boat and began walking on the water. When he looked down and saw the wind and waves swirling about his feet, he became fearful and started to sink. Jesus reached out his hand and caught him asking, "You of little faith, why did you doubt?" When they climbed into the boat, immediately the wind died down and they reached the other side. (Matthew 14: 25-33)

On a good day, Peter seemed filled with heavenly inspiration and revelation, but on a bad day he bumbled along as a stumbling block. Perhaps that is why, he is so relatable. Those who point fingers at Peter and gawk and can't relate probably haven't walked the Christian life long enough.

After all these miracles signs and wonders, Jesus asked Peter a question, "So, what about you? Who do you say I am?" Peter stuttered a safe reply, "Some say, John the Baptist; others say Elijah; and still others, Jeremiah or one of the prophets. Jesus pressed the big fisherman, "But who do you say I am?" Thoughtfully Simon Peter replied, "You are the Christ, the Son of the living God!"

Soon Peter would be tested far beyond what even he could imagine. In an upper room, the disciples were hustling about getting everything ready for Passover. Jesus, as unconventional as ever, shocked all those present by taking the position of the lowest slave and washing their dirty, dusty feet before supper. He reminded them that He would be with them only a little while longer. Peter upset and confused protested, this time loudly and demanded to know why he could not follow his Master.

> "Lord, where are you going?" asked Peter
> Jesus replied, "Where I am going, you cannot follow now, but you will follow later."
> Peter said to Him, "Lord, why can't I follow you now? I will lay down my life for you."
> Jesus answered, "Will you really lay down your life for me? I tell you the truth, before the rooster crows, you will disown me three times!" John 13:36-38. (NET)

The Crowing Rooster

After their Passover meal, Jesus prayed in the Garden of Gethsemane, and then the night further deteriorated. Soldiers wanted to arrest Jesus but Peter tried to protect Him by drawing his sword. He only managed to slice off the ear of Malchus. Jesus rebuked him. "Peter, put your sword away! Shall I not drink the cup the Father has given Me?" After He miraculously restored the ear back on Malchus, He was taken to the high priest to be beaten, tried and then sentenced to death. Peter and John followed Jesus to the High Priest's courtyard at a safe distance. Hovering in the shadows, around the fire, Peter's Galilean accent was picked up and he was asked about his association with Jesus. Peter vigorously denied he knew Jesus. Two more times Peter was asked if he knew Jesus. This time he swore and shouted back at a small girl, "I never knew him!" At that precise moment the rooster crowed fulfilling Jesus' prediction of denial by Peter. Realizing he had broken his oath to his friend, Peter wept bitterly, tore his clothes and fled from the scene into the night. His friend needed him, but Peter was nowhere to be found. Then Jesus was crucified on the cross. Just when things seemed as though they could not get worse, they did. It is hard to be judgmental of the big fisherman. After all, given similar circumstances what would you or I have done? Ashamed and confused, Peter abandoned the ministry and returned to the one thing he could be sure about, fishing. It is interesting to note the other disciples did not fare much better as only half of them continued to follow Him. But even though Peter abandoned Jesus, He had not abandoned Peter. After Jesus was raised from the dead and before His ascension into heaven, Jesus found and appeared to His friend Peter and restored him in an amazing account of forgiveness.

Simon Peter led fellow apostles Thomas, Nathaniel, the Zebedee brothers (John and James) and all went fishing. Toiling all night they caught nothing. An unknown man stood afar on the distant shore of the Tiberius Sea and called out to them and asked a familiar question.

Jesus shouted "Friends have you caught anything?"

"No," they answered.

"Throw your net on the right side of the boat and you will find some." John 21:5&6. (CEV)

Obediently, Peter threw his net on the other side of the boat. The catch of fish was so large he had to get help from his friends. It was good to struggle with such bounty as they laughed to each other and pulled in the haul. Suddenly Peter remembered, Jesus used the same statement and even the identical miracle when He first called Peter. He clothed himself and leaped into the water to swim ashore. But the closer he got to shore, the more he thought about all those horrifying events of the past few days. Conflicted, he climbed ashore and began to count the fish, slowly! "One hundred and fifty three fish," he proudly announced smiling and held up the last fish in his hand for everyone to see. Then Jesus took the bread, blessed it and gave it to the men as He had done so many times before.

No one asked who it was because when He broke the bread, everyone knew who it was. It felt good to be with the Master again as the hungry disciples consumed the fresh fish and inhaled the freshly baked bread. When they finished eating, Jesus looked up at Peter. You could have heard a pin drop as time stood still and the scene unfolded before the men, His men. Jesus asked Peter:

"Simon, son of John, do you truly love me more than these?"

"Yes, Lord," Peter said softly, "You know that I love you."

Jesus then said to Peter, "Feed my lambs." Again Jesus said, "Simon, son of John, do you truly love me?"

He answered, "Yes, Lord, you know that I love you."

Jesus said, "Take care of my sheep." The third time Jesus said, "Simon son of John, do you love me?"

Peter vexed with grief because Jesus asked him a third time, "Do you love me?" shouted and implored, "Lord, you know all things: you know that I love you."

Jesus said, "Then feed my sheep." (John 21)

Day of Pentecost

A joyful Peter, with tears streaming down his face, was now fully reinstated and restored and resumed his rightful place of leadership. He had learned a valuable lesson, that in his own ability he could never be faithful no matter how much he declared it to be so. Without the help of the Lord, he could only manage one quality decision, "Yes, Lord, I do love You, Jesus."

Jesus had called Peter, Cephas or Rock, and promised to build His church upon His teachings and reminded them that the gates of hell would not prevail against it. This was not about a building but about a community of believers. With the indwelling Holy Spirit, Peter now could be faithful. So it is with us, "He knows the way I take and when he has tested me, I will come forth as gold." Job 23:10. Then Jesus gave the men their final instructions.

> "Do not leave Jerusalem but wait for the gift my Father promised, which you have heard me speak about. For John baptized with water but in a few days you will be baptized with the Holy Spirit." Acts 1:4, 5. (NKJV)

On the day of Pentecost, the disciples and followers of Jesus waited in an upper room in Jerusalem. Not sure of what they were waiting for, they prayed until the event occurred and then no questions were necessary.

> When they arrived, they went upstairs to the room where they were staying. Those present were Peter, John, James and Andrew; Philip and Thomas, Bartholomew and

35

Matthew, James son of Alpheus and Simon the Zealot, and Judas son of James. They all joined together constantly in prayer, along with the women and Mary the mother of Jesus and with his brethren. Acts 1: 12-14. (NIV)

When the day of Pentecost came, they were together in one place. Suddenly a sound like the blowing of a violent wind came from heaven & filled the whole house where they were sitting. They saw what seemed to be tongues of fire that separated and came to rest on each of them. All of them were filled with the Holy Spirit and began to speak in other tongues as the Spirit enabled them. Acts 2:1-4. (NIV)

The group became so loud that Jews gathered below from the Feast of Pentecost and began to ask questions, thinking the disciples were drunk. Peter, filled with the Holy Spirit, addressed the crowd.

Fellow Jews and all of you who live in Jerusalem, let me explain this to you; listen carefully to what I say. These men are not drunk as you suppose. It is only nine in the morning! No this is what was spoken by the prophet Joel. In the last days, I will pour out my Spirit on all people. Acts 2:14-17. (NIV)

Then Peter and the other apostles transformed by the power of the Holy Spirit performed many miraculous signs, healing wonders among the people.

As a result, people brought the sick into the streets, laid them on beds and mats so that at least Peters shadow might fall on some of them as he passed by. Acts 5:15. (Berean)

It was later Peter who discerned that it was God's will for the gentile population to be saved and filled with the Holy Ghost just as the Jews had been.

> While Peter was still speaking these words, the Holy Spirit came on all who heard the message. The circumcised believers who had come with Peter were astonished that the gift of the Holy Spirit had been poured out even on the Gentiles. For they heard them speaking in tongues and praising God." Peter said, "Can anyone keep these people from being baptized with water? They received the Holy Ghost just as we have." So he ordered that they be baptized (in water) in the name of Jesus Christ. Acts 10:44-48. (NIV)

The Apostle Peter transformed by Holy Spirit on the Day of Pentecost is an example to follow for all who believe in and name Jesus Christ as their Lord. In the Old Testament only the super heroes of faith had the Holy Spirit, but in the New Testament all believers had the ability to be filled with the Holy Spirit and speak in tongues as the Spirit gave them utterance. As individuals yield and submit themselves to the plan of God, the Spirit rebuilds that person from the inside out and transforms us into the image of Jesus Christ just like the Apostle Peter.

I know firsthand because when I was in college, I attended a church that didn't believe in the various manifestations of the Holy Spirit. However, one friend, Annie, always looked radiant as if she had swallowed a light bulb. When I asked her why she always glowed, she invited me to her Bible study where they laid hands on me to be filled with the Holy Spirit. It wasn't until two days later that speaking in tongues manifested. God's timing is perfect.

The following teaching from Derek Prince tells us how to receive the Holy Spirit with the manifestation of speaking in tongues. A person must be thirsty, feel ill-equipped and inadequate to live this life alone and, as Peter did, realize their need for more of God. Jesus said there are three impossible things, 1) to please God without faith 2) for God to lie and 3) for the blood of bulls and goats to take away sin. Are you ready to yield and take the next step to receive power to live a successful Christian life? If you believe and have faith, God will give you the gift of the Holy Spirit as He promised.

Remember the following:

1. "All that the Father gives will come to Me, and whoever comes to me I will never cast out." John 6:37. (English Std.)

2. You have to drink in the Spirit. God will never override your free will. You have to open your physical being (mouth) and breathe in. If you do your part, God will do His part.

3. You must release the outflow, through your mouth in speech. Then the Holy Ghost will give you this supernatural infilling. (Luke 11) If you ask for the right thing, you will never get the wrong thing.

4. Remember you are doing the speaking, but God is giving the words.

Scripture Declarations:

1. And this water symbolizes baptism that now saves you also not the removal of dirt from the body but the pledge of a good conscience toward God. I Peter 3:21. (NIV)

2. "Therefore go and make disciples of all nations, baptizing them in the name of the Father and of the Son and of the Holy Spirit, and teaching them to obey everything I have commanded you.

And surely I am with you always, to the end of the age. Matthew 28: 19-20. (NIV)

Questions:

1. What is the difference between water baptism and being filled with the Holy Spirit?

2. Name one miracle that Jesus did as a result of being filled with the Holy Spirit.

3. Name a disciple who walked away from ministry but was later restored by an encounter with Jesus.

Action Goals

1. Have you been baptized? If not you may want to make an appointment to do so.

2. Have you followed the steps of being filled with the Holy Spirit? If not, you may want to do so.

Declaration/Prayer:

Today I make a commitment to be baptized in water. I remember that when I enter the water I do so in remembrance of your death on the cross and when I come up out of the waters of baptism, I emerge as a brand new person who is committed to take the journey of renewing my emotions so that I can become a healthy person one step at a time. Lord Jesus I also come to you as my baptizer in the Holy Spirit. I present my body to be used as a temple of the Holy Spirit and my tongue to be used as an instrument of righteousness. By faith I receive and thank you for this gift in the Name of Jesus. Now I give you my voice. Caution: The accuser of the brethren Satan will say that when you begin to speak in tongues, you are just making this up. Just command him to go in the name of Jesus and he will flee.

Today, I am sealed in His precious blood and filled with the Holy Spirit. Today, I am an overcomer and nothing will be impossible for me because my heavenly Father has given His seal of the Holy Spirit as an endorsement on my life. Today, Jesus has delegated power and authority in His name to me as His disciple and because of this I can teach, preach and demonstrate His kingdom by casting out demons, raising the dead and healing the sick. Thank you for baptizing me in the Holy Spirit.

Chapter Notes

CHAPTER FOUR

FINDING AND YIELDING TO A GOD GIVEN VISION

As newlyweds, my husband and I were given the opportunity to stay at a cottage on a lake. Rick grew up in Michigan and his parents had a lake cottage, so I assumed he was an experienced fisherman. One a particular day, Rick decided to take me fishing so we could "catch" our supper. As a city girl, I knew nothing about fishing but I eagerly watched him bait a line and cast it expertly into the shimmering lake. Floundering (no pun intended) a little, I tried to impale Squishy the worm on the line, but it took a lot more time than expected. Not realizing that my husband had moved behind me, I cast the line backwards and heard an anguishing yell. Without realizing it, I had cast my line into Rick's t-shirt. He stormed up to me and snatched the line away from me with choice words under his breath implying my casting days were over.

"Why didn't you look where you were casting?" he implored.

Sheepishly, I ducked my head not knowing what to say. Honestly the thought never occurred to me. Not a good omen for what would soon transpire.

Now Rick was the person solely responsible for getting our supper. His line floated aimlessly for what seemed like an eternity as we waited for a fish to bite. As I grew hungrier various thoughts popped into my mind like. How can people say this fun and relaxing? Which quickly disintegrated into, Catch the stupid fish already! The fish in the lake seemed to be in no hurry to cooperate as the sun sunk lower and lower into West. Finally, Rick landed a beautiful, foot long bass.

"At last, supper will soon be on the grill," I suggested helpfully as Rick proceeded to take the hook out of the fish's mouth. After he made the fatal mistake of dropping the fish on the shore beside me, he began to shout and wave his arms, "Grab the fishing net, grab the net!" But I was too inexperienced and slow to understand the implications of his frantic moves. Splish, splash, the huge fish wiggled and jumped from shoreline right back in the water and quickly jetted away. We had only been married about six months and my sweet tempered husband was revealing a side of himself that I had never seen before. Our blissful happy state of marriage was being put to the test by a fish!

To add insult to injury, the neighbor next door had quietly appeared, probably because of all the yelling and placed his rod and reel in the water just a few of feet away from us. Moments later he successfully hauled in our fish. In no uncertain terms, I told my husband to march over and get our fish but my husband refused. I folded my arms over my chest but Rick wouldn't budge no matter how hard I pouted. We sat down to a peanut butter and jelly sandwich that evening.

> My frame was not hidden from you, when I was woven together in the depths of the earth, your eyes saw my unformed body, all the days ordained for me were written in your book, before one of them came to be. Psalm 139:15, 16. (NIV)

Knowing Your Purpose

Fishing for a purpose in life can be as equally exasperating as the fish story I just told you. You hope that those written goals will translate into a set of positive outcomes. Unless you and the group to which you have attached yourself knows what they are doing, then all of you will end up empty handed at the end of your life with nothing to show for all the effort.

God has placed eternity in each person's heart. If we want to spend eternity with Creator God in heaven we must choose a relationship with Him while we have breath in our bodies here on earth. Furthermore if we believe this statement is true then shouldn't we be asking Him for direction in our lives, guidance for all our decisions, and wisdom for each day to carry it out.

Rick Warren wrote a best-selling devotional book called *The Purpose Driven Life*. It topped *Wall Street Journal* best seller charts, selling more than 30 million copies by 2007 and then was on the *New York Times* best-selling list for the next 90 weeks. From these statistics, one can assume that people would like to know why they are here and what they are supposed to do with their lives. Warren's book gives his reader a 40 day personal spiritual journey where five God given purposes are a "blueprint" for daily Christian living. They include the following: People are planned for a purpose, formed for God's family, created to become like Christ, shaped for serving God, and finally, made for a mission.

Warren begins his book with the words, "It is not about you! It is all about God." He claims that if a person wants to know what purpose they were created for, then they must consult "Creator God" along with His manual, the Bible. Only then will a person discover the true reason of why they have been placed on the earth. Warren contends that if a person tries to "invent" their purpose by acquiring things, possessions or yielding power over others, by the end of life they are going to feel as though their lives were futile. The life of a Christian begins with a person named Jesus, but it must be consummated with the nature of Jesus in our heart, attitudes, pursuits and in our actions.

The Lord has made everything for His purpose. Proverbs 16:4. (Berean)

Warren also states that only God knows the complete details of a person's life, because He was looking on before that person began to breathe and even watched their hidden parts being knit together. God knows how many days we would have on earth and has even scheduled what each day should look like. In John Bevere's book *Driven by Eternity,* numerous details are given about how we should prioritize our lives, and then concludes with the Judgment Seat of Christ, where Jesus will decide rewards based on how our life has been aligned with His purposes.

> Long before God laid down the earth's foundation, He had us in mind. Ephesians. 1:4. (MSG)

According to Warren, it makes no difference who you are or where you come from if you want God and are ready to do what he asks, then the door is open to you. In the beginning of this chapter, an example was given of two inexperienced fishermen, my husband and me. Now I am going to give an example of one of our church elders who is a fantastic fisherman. His name is Bucky and he leaves nothing to chance. When Bucky, along with friends Carl and Dennis prepare to go fishing they begin by asking the Lord's guidance. Then they check their equipment, the weather, the tides, what fish are biting, and how many can be legally caught, and lastly what bait is most tantalizing. There is no guessing with these guys. When casting times comes, this crew's intentional preparation lands them with coolers full of fresh fish. When they do their part and ask God to do His, then they experience a net breaking, boat sinking, load of fish.

> For I know the plans I have for you," declares the Lord. "They are plans for your good and not for disaster, to give you hope and a future." Jeremiah 29:11. (NLT)

God has a wonderful plan for each of our lives and He wants us to be successful in what we do. Therefore when vision casting for a God given purpose, make appropriate preparations by being less sensitive to the world and more sensitive to what God wants for your life. Worship, listen and make God and His word live within you as the priority and the authority of your life. Go to Him daily in prayer and find a suitable daily Bible reading plan. Some suggest reading one chapter in the Old Testament and one chapter in the New Testament, while others like to read a book of the Bible in a designated time frame, or take a chapter in Psalms or Proverbs for each day of the week. Having a pen and highlighter along with a notebook is a good idea to write down or underline when the Holy Spirit emphasizes a word, phrase or even verse that seems to jump off the pages of your Bible.

Sometimes I read and reread a passage but nothing seems to strike me, but like the steady drip, drip, drip of raindrops under a water spout, eventually my cup of understanding will fill up. So it is with meditation. As I think about the scripture, the truth seems to leap off the page bringing clarity, encouragement and understanding to my mind. By dating and then writing an explanation about the passage, I can make a plan of action as a reminder about want I need to do.

Apostle Peter Finishes His Journey

When we return to study the life of the Apostle Peter we notice that he still had another important task to complete his life's journey thus fulfilling his destiny. After Peter's baptism in the Holy Spirit, he was even more powerful than when he walked with Jesus. Past failures did not disqualify him for the ministry but rather repentance, sanctification and obedience qualified him for the ministry. What would have happened if Peter had not humbled himself, yielded and been willingly restored to leadership? What would have happened to the rest of the disciples? Surely the church in Acts would have looked very different. Church tradition records that the persecution of Christians in Rome became so intense that the early church encouraged Peter to take the Appian Road out of the city. But as Peter took to the road to leave Rome he had a vision from Jesus and asked the Savior an important question in Latin, *"Quo Vadis, Domine,"* or "where are you going Lord?" Jesus replied, "Back to Rome to be crucified again." Perhaps it was then that Peter remembered the final words of Jesus.

> "I tell you the truth, when you were young you dressed yourself and went where you wanted to go; but when you are old you will stretch out your hands, and others will dress you and take you where you do not want to go." Jesus said this to indicate the kind of death by which Peter would glorify God. John 21: 18, 19. (NLT)

Then He said to him "Follow me!"

Tradition tells us that Peter turned around and headed back into Rome to encourage his fellow believers who were being burned alive, crucified, fed and destroyed by wild animals in Nero's circus. Peter felt unworthy to be crucified as His Lord was, so he asked to be crucified upside down. After Peter's crucifixion, his body was dumped like discarded refuse across the Tiber River. Like a precious seed, his shed blood nourished the faith of those early believers and became a place that Christian pilgrims not only venerated but also visited as a holy site. Today a red granite obelisk that once marked Nero's Roman circus stands with a cross on top to mark the entry way to the basilica of St. Peter in the Vatican City where Peter's discarded body was tossed. Church history tells us that far below the central chapel altar of St Peter Basilica in the Vatican City in Rome, Italy is another altar in the shape of an upside down cross. Inside the altar there is a small box that has been verified to contain the remains of a robust man in his sixties from the first century. The church believes the identified remains are of the Apostle Peter.

> "And I tell you that you are Peter, and on this rock I will build my church, and the gates of hell shall not prevail against it. And I will give you the keys of the kingdom of heaven; whatever you bind on earth will be bound in

heaven and whatever you loose on earth will be loosed in heaven." Matthew 16:18, 19 (ESV)

Rick Warren states that in order to become a mature Christian believer we must know and adhere to Purpose 3 which is to become a disciple of Christ and connect to other believers. By study, sharing, fellowship, and accountability, we can assist and pray for each other and encourage each other during times of trial. In serving, caring and watching out for each other we become more Christ like.

All scripture is God-breathed and is useful for teaching, rebuking, correcting and training in righteousness, so that the servant of God may be thoroughly equipped for every good work. II Timothy 3:16. (NIV)

Abraham's Purpose: A Journey with God

Living in obedience and yielding to Christ as His disciple means being willing to take a journey that begins with God. In the book of Genesis, we find a man called Abraham who loved God so much that he left the comfort of his home, Ur of the Chaldees or modern day Iraq, and traveled to a far country called Canaan simply because God asked him to. This promise from God eventually included possessing the Promised Land through Abraham's descendants which included the nation of Israel, which in turn produced our Savior, the Lord Jesus Christ. According to the New Testament, Abraham was our example of being a friend to God who was loved by Him, communed with Him and trusted Him by following the directions and purpose God had for his life. In turn, Abraham was blessed exceedingly and called Father of our faith.

God promised Abraham a land for his descendants to possess which may have seemed a bewildering statement to make because in reality it was an impossible task for Abraham and his wife to have children. His wife Sarai was barren. Furthermore the two were getting along in age or to put it delicately "well past the productive years". Our story begins in Genesis 12: 1-3, As a result of Abraham's covenant with God, his name was changed from Abram meaning "Father is exalted" to Abraham meaning "Father of a multitude" (Genesis 17). This seemed to be a silly name given the fact the couple had no children. At one point Abraham and Sarai decided to help out God and took matters into their own hands by having Abraham sleep with Sarai's maid Hagar. As a result of the union, Hagar became pregnant with a boy she named Ismael. Ismael became the delight of his father Abraham, causing competition and enmity to rage between the slave girl Hagar and her mistress Sarai. The legal heir and son, Ismael would one day inherit everything from his father, so Hagar had a preferred position in the clan.

God never intended his promised nation to come from a child born of a slave concubine. Rather, He wanted the child to come from Abraham's legal wife Sarai. Eventually, God supernaturally intervened and sent an angel, and Sarai's name was changed to Sarah signifying her relationship with God. Her 90 year-old body was reinvigorated as she gave birth to Isaac (translation laughter) who became the father of Jacob who eventually became Israel. This fulfilled the promise God gave Abraham way back in Genesis 15:5 about descendants as numerous as the stars.

> Then he brought him outside and said, "Look now toward sky and count the stars, if you are able to number them; and he said to him, so shall your descendants be. Genesis 15:5. (NKJV)

Lessons from History: Wilberforce

There are numerous examples from history where someone has yielded to God for the plan and purpose of their life. William Wilberforce was an English politician and philanthropist who lived from 1739 to 1833. After his conversion to Christ, as Wilberforce read and studied the Bible, he realized that slavery was against God's moral laws. He decided to devote his life to the cause of abolition. In his day, slavery was an intricately woven into the economy, culture and society of Great Britain. For Wilberforce scripture took precedence over the cultural norms of his time so he devoted his life to its implementation.

Despite intense criticism from peers, for the next twenty-six years of his life, Wilberforce worked tirelessly, sacrificially, and fought to legally abolish slavery in England. Finally, three days before his death, with his health broken, he saw the passage of the Slavery Abolition Act of 1833 which abolished slavery in the entire British Empire.

Modern Day Hero of Faith: Christine Caine

Another individual committed to fulfilling her God given purpose and leaving a legacy for future generations is Christine Caine. This amazing woman created a team whose sole purpose is to rescue others. She travels the world, speaking with passion on behalf of voiceless victims: women caught in the web of human trafficking. Christine herself was a victim of sexual abuse. Christine Caine came from a Greek immigrant family in Australia and from the age of three to fifteen she endured sexually molestation from four men. In her own words, she was used for a purpose that she was never designed for. On the outside she seemed like an over achiever and happy, but inside she carried shame, bitterness, anger, guilt and unforgiveness. Then one day, she became a Christian, but soon she realized that she would never fulfill her God given destiny unless she chose to own her past sexual abuse as sin. As she diligently studied God's word and allowed it to penetrate deep within her soul, the stronghold that sin had over her was broken and she was finally free from the tormenting memories of the past. She said she thought she would never stop weeping. After many hours, she arose from that experience cleansed from the emotional scars on her soul and was able to forgive those who had sinned against her. When she finally found release, Christine was able to embrace the future God had for her. Her past no longer dictated her future.

This wounded individual who God rescued created a team that is now rescuing others. Christine and her husband Nick founded The A21 Campaign, an anti-human trafficking organization with a goal to abolish slavery in the 21st century just as Wilberforce had so many centuries earlier. These two individuals embody Purpose 4 and 5 of Rick Warren's book that says, we were born for a ministry and a mission. Like Wilberforce, Christine Caine is passionate about social justice, and wants to make a difference in her generation. Her organization has offices around the world that actively rescue the innocent and bring perpetrators to justice. Like her name sake so many centuries earlier she was once a castaway and is now illuminating Christ to a lost and broken world. Instead of cursing the darkness, Christine is serving her generation, lighting a candle, one person at a time and leaving a legacy of faith for future generations.

Scriptures:

1. For we are God's workmanship, created in Christ Jesus to do good works, which God has before ordained that we should do them. Ephesians 2:10. (Berean)

2. Therefore whoever hears these sayings of mine and doeth them, I will liken him unto a wise man, which built his house upon a rock: and the rain descended and the floods came, and the winds blew and beat upon that house; and it fell not: for it was founded upon a rock. And every one that hears these sayings of mine, and doeth them not, shall be liken unto a foolish man, which built his house upon a sand: And the rain descended, and the floods came, and the winds blew, and beat upon that house; and it fell: and great was the fall of it. Matthew 7:24-27. (KJV)

Questions

1. If a person would like to know what their purpose is, how would they go about finding it?

2. What person, from the Old Testament, had a God-given vision for their life?

3. According to Rick Warren what are five God-given purposes for daily living?

4. Give the name of a past or modern day hero and write down how they fulfilled their purpose.

Action Goals

1. Start a journal and ask God to reveal the purpose for your life. Write down what you believe it is.

2. Begin by praying and ask God to give you an accompanying scripture that speaks to you regarding your purpose. Write it down here and begin praying daily for the people you will reach.

3. Are there any obstacles that are keeping you from moving forward? If so, write down what they are.

Confession/Prayer

Dear God,

Thank you for creating me. I will attend to your word and by meditation and worship and praise (Purpose 1). I will remember that You delight in me and that I am made in Your image and you placed me in your family

(*Purpose 2*). I will put aside my own plans for this day and for the rest of my life choose to focus on the plans and tasks that You (*Purpose 3*) have for me. Please reveal Your purpose for this day so it is meaningful and fulfilled and reveal the purpose that You have created me for. Lord, help me to open my eyes and see opportunities in front of me (*Purpose 4*) as I obey Matthew 10: 8 and what it says, "Heal the sick, cleanse the lepers, raise the dead and cast out demons. Freely you have received, freely give."

I will not allow past pain to destroy and dictate my future (*Purpose 5*). I make the decision here and now to willingly forgive any and all those who have sinned against me. Father God, thank you for cleansing and healing my wounded soul from painful past memories that would hinder my forward progress. Thank you Jesus, Thank you Holy Spirit, Amen.

Chapter Notes

CHAPTER FIVE

HEALTHY CHURCH COMMUNITIES

Jesus told the disciples that it was better for Him to go away, because once He became a sin offering, the Holy Spirit could reside within mankind. Only by the cleansing of His blood will our human vessel be sufficiently clean for Holy Spirit's occupation. The Holy Spirit can now give an individual wisdom to verbally witness, and then power to demonstrate living a successful Christian life. Now, nothing is impossible for the follower of Christ to believe, confess, and to do. When Jesus was on the earth, He was limited by an earthly shell, his human body. He could only be in one place at one time.

When Jesus left earth, He ushered in a new dispensation which called for the infilling of the Holy Spirit and created the Church Age. For the disciples in the Book of Acts, it meant that everywhere they were the works of Jesus could be demonstrated by them, not just in one person, not just in Israel, but in all of Christ's disciples at the same time. For us today, it means that everywhere we are, He is!

As staggering as this is to imagine, consider the possibilities that exist if the children of God know who they are, and relinquish control, allowing the kingdom of God through their spirits, souls and bodies to invade the earth exponentially. Empowered by His Spirit, a disciple of Christ can be more influential than any worldly conqueror because Jesus is in all of His disciples who make the decision to yield to the Holy Spirit.

"If you love me, you will obey what I command. And I will ask the Father, and He will give you another Counselor to be with you forever - the Spirit of Truth. The world cannot accept him, because it neither sees him nor knows him. But you know Him, for He lives with you and will be in you. I will not leave you as orphans; I will come to you. Before long, the world will not see me anymore, but you will see me. Because I live, you also will live. On that day you will realize that I am in my Father and you are in me, and I am in you." John 14:15-20. (NIV)

Rudy's Gym: Accountability and Success

An important aspect of church life is accountability. A while ago, I had a knee injury. I wasn't aware of the extent of the injury until I took a family trip to New Orleans with my husband and daughter. Usually, my daughter Grace and I wear my husband out by all day shopping all over town, but on this trip in a very short time I was out of breath, stopping every couple of minutes with my right knee in constant pain. My daughter noticed my limping and pointed it out, but instead of being grateful I was defensive. Nagging in the back of my mind was the thought I am getting older. How does she expect me to keep up with her when she is half my age? Clearly, Grace was the problem. Deep inside, I knew that these were excuses for me being out of shape and carrying an extra twenty pounds of weight. Right then and there I made a quality determination to make an appointment with my physical therapist, Rudy.

However, one appointment with Rudy was not going make up for months of neglect and for a calf muscle that had shrunk nearly an entire inch (he had measured the right calf and compared it with my left calf muscle). When I committed to a workout program, my daughter suggested that perhaps I should take off a couple of pounds! It was as though we had changed places: she was now the mom and I was the daughter, it was an unhappy prospect. My family encouraged me to continue working with Rudy and not quit! When Rudy put me on a strengthening and conditioning regimen, the inch of calf muscle slowly began to return. In reality it took about a year and a lot of hard work. It was wonderful getting stronger and having more endurance to go from one end of Home Depot to the other. I still battled with emotions and there were plenty of days when I was looking for excuses not to go to the gym and exercise, but being able to be active again was worth it all.

Sometimes Rudy would demonstrate a new exercise and he could tell by the disapproving are you kidding look on my face that I was about to verbalize something negative. Rudy would then remind me not to verbalize the complaint as that would undermine what I was trying to do. In other words, don't let the ear hear what the mind thought, otherwise the body would chime in and agree, "We can't do this!"

"Never whine, grumble or complain until you have tried it a couple of times, Eileen." Rudy encouraged before, during or after hard work outs. He never berated our sessions or told me they should have gone better. He corrected my thought process, by positive verbalization and ongoing accountability that was critical to a successful outcome. Rudy called it the battle of the mind. "The destination will take care of itself if each step in the journey is carefully and intentionally planned."

Another important aspect of training in the gym was the people I worked out with, like Sue who would text me to check and make sure I was coming to workout. There were club members of like mind who were committed to keeping healthy. One of Rudy's favorite Bible verses:

I can do all things through Christ who strengthens me. Philippians 4:13. (KJV)

The Bible has given us many examples that reveal how much our Creator God understands the weakness and predisposition of an individual's heart and attitude to negativity. After Adam sinned in the garden, his flesh ruled him rather than his Spirit. As our Spirits become healthy and strong, they should edit and control our thought life rather than the flesh. Scripture reminds us to pull down every thought that acknowledges itself against God. In other words; be determined to stick with and obey God's word. With the help of the Holy Spirit, we can overcome past challenges and bad habits of the flesh.

Years ago, I was diagnosed with kidney failure and could have died. My written testimony and journey with the steps to overcoming sickness and returning to health are featured in my book, *Out of the Belly of the Whale*. At first I was in denial: this can't be happening to me. Then I was angry with God: how could YOU let this happen to me? Finally I was not even sure I would ever be well again. By diligently studying God's Word I realized that God made a provision for me to be free from sickness. A huge part of my overcoming journey included not just revelations from the Lord but encouragement from my immediate and extended family. I also had constant prayer and support from the body of Christ to pursue, overtake and recover. Seeking God diligently, I allowed Him to confront and correct areas of my life that did not line up with His word. In short I had to change my "stinking thinking!" Hearing positive messages from preachers and ongoing encouragement from family members and my sisters and brothers in Christ helped me when progress seemed at a snail's pace or perhaps test results revealed my body was not improving. At just the right time, someone would call, come over, hand me a message or a tape of a preacher that kept me moving forward until I was well.

There were many days when I felt as though I would never overcome this or that particular battle. Other times, life felt like a battleground of confusion where my belief system was being turned inside out, but I held tenaciously onto faith with the Lord and in the end He helped me to prevail and realize my goal of physical health. It is the same with emotional health. An individual cannot be full of pride, refuse the help of others, and be unwilling to admit they need adjustments in their thinking. Sometimes even sessions with a counselor are needed.

Martin Luther, leader of the protestant reformation in the Middle Ages, defined the church as a community of saints, comprised of holy persons under the head of (Jesus Christ), collected by the Spirit, with one faith, one mind, endowed with gifts but united in love and absent of sects and divisions. In Greek, the church is the word *Ekklesia* meaning "called out ones" coming from a broader community to a smaller one, for the "purpose of living life in the Spirit."

> But you are a chosen race, a royal priesthood, a holy nation, a people of God's own possession, that might proclaim the excellency of Him who called you out of darkness into his marvelous light. I Peter 2:9. (ESV)

Church life may seem a strange and daunting task for a new believer. In the early 1980's, Rick accepted a job that moved our family to a rural part of the country. As a city girl I thought the prospect of living next to chickens, pigs and cows seemed idyllic. In reality, I didn't realize how many adjustments that we would have to make. You can take the girl out of the city but it may be a challenge to take the city out of the girl. Differences in clothing, attitudes about education, food, and communicating were obstacles, but Rick and I knew our family needed to stay involved and accountable to a healthy church body. This was a non-negotiable for us. Proverbs states that in the multitude of counselors, there is wisdom. Neither did we check our brains at the door, but like the Bereans in Acts we kept checking to see if what was taught in church measured up against what God's Word said, and we used discernment in developing friendships. In the end the experience proved to be a positive one, because we learned so much about ourselves and learned to love others who were culturally different. Believers need to tenaciously stick with the church world even when it feels strange if they expect to keep growing.

Do not forsake the assembling of ourselves together, as is the manner of some, but exhorting one another and so much the more (especially) as ye see the Day approaching. Hebrews 10:25. (NKJV)

While preparing to write this chapter, I began looking at Internet sites that talked about the characteristics of a healthy church, and there were many things to consider but certain points seem to come up repeatedly. 1) Teaching of the scripture must be paramount and should be taught in an expository fashion. The pastor doesn't use scripture for back up about what he thinks or for his own agenda. Rather he studies to show himself approved before God and to amplify the true meaning of the scriptures for the believers. A preacher's teaching should be subject to the text and not the other way. 2) The Israelites and the early church devoted themselves to prayer. Therefore members must be taught how to pray and praise and then given the opportunity to serve with their gifts in the community. This allows God to encourage, teach, touch, heal and perform signs and wonders to the people directly. 3) There must be a clear discipleship path so the members understand, reflect and adjust their lives according to the teaching of the Bible and grow in their faith. 4) Members must be known, accountable, loved and allowed to break bread together in sub-groups that allow them to identify, develop and serve and help each other with their spiritual gifts. 5) There should be racial, gender, cultural and economic diversity that reflects the community where the church is located.

They devoted themselves to the Apostle's teaching, to the fellowship, to the breaking of bread and prayer. Acts 2:42 (NIV)

When studying scripture we notice that human beings encounter difficulty in life, but sometimes it is also our furry, fellow creatures that we share the planet with that may need a helping hand. After all, didn't Jesus say,

"Whatever you did for one of the least of these brothers and sisters of mine, you did it for Me." Matthew 25:40. (CSB)

Christ also reminds us in Ephesians that as He is the head of the church, we are His body. This means that each of us is tasked with being His compassionate hands, heart, voice, etc. So what does saving a stray kitten have to do with church life? Everything! The church is a community of believers, sometimes called 'brethren' who accept individuals into an environment where the participant grows to the point where they become healthy contributing members of that community. If corrective measures are needed, because someone has been neglected, sinned or gotten tangled in error, then they should be lovingly corrected and welcomed back into the fold.

The Trials of Marco the Kitten

One steamy, humid summer evening in Florida, the temperature was running about ninety five degrees. A cozy house on the Hillsborough River was attracting buzzing mosquitoes large enough to carry off little babies. Not really true, but I was just taking some literary license and decided to borrow a line from Peter Falk's popular movie *The In-Laws.* Now back to our story, as I was saying, it was a hot summer night and Joy our younger daughter was relaxing on her lanai listening to the usual cacophony of crickets and tree frogs. Somewhere in the distance, she heard a desperate fight for survival playing out between predator and prey. Coincidently, she noticed that a closer and tiny meow seemed to be coming from a nearby bush. Carefully, Joy meowed back a soft response into the bushes where the creature seemed to be.

For the next hour multiple meows passed back and forth between Joy and the little creature in distress. Joy decided to drop some little pieces of cat food down in the general vicinity of a bush where she thought the noise was coming from. From the blackness and to her amazement, a tiny, wobbly kitten emerged from the greenery. Cautiously, the dirty gray bundle gobbled up the pieces of food but quickly scampered back to safety when Joy tried to move closer. Fearful that the frightened bundle would not survive the night and would meet a similar fate of whatever had happened across the street, Joy made a compassionate decision. Laying down a trail of the cat food, she continued to coax Marco out - appropriately named for the game she had been playing with him. The trail of the scattered tidbits led straight to the open door of her screened lanai. Distrustfully, the cautious stranger followed the delightful morsels until it was safely inside. Joy quickly slammed the screen door shut trapping the tabby kitten. And so it was on a steamy summer night that a kitten named Marco staggered in and found sanctuary from a compassionate heart.

"For the Son of man came to seek and to save the lost." Luke 19:10. (NIV)

Marco Finds a Home

Days passed and as I heard about Marco's progress, I decided it was time for a visit so we arranged a lunch date. Joy warned me not to expect too much from Marco and gave me very specific directions about my actions during the visit.

"Mom you can come over, but know that Marco is still very skittish and cannot be picked up or handled. He distrusts everyone." She further explained that only yesterday was she able to set the food out and watch Marco eat but as soon as he finished his meal, he quickly scampered away." Marco had been rescued, but he was still in survival mode.

With incredible patience, Joy had Marco litter box trained but he was still had a long way to go before any family would adopt him. After all people would expect a friendly and cuddly kitten not some wild, independent stray that just consumed food on the back porch and skittered away after being fed. Finally the day arrived for my visit. Joy ushered me out to the screen porch where I was to sit in a lawn chair like a granite statue, quietly.

Barely breathing, Joy called out softly, "Marco", then again, "Marco," and put out treats for him on the cement floor. Soon, we began to hear strange creaking movements coming from the grill. Was I in a scene from *A Christmas Carol* with the ghost of Christmas past? Gingerly poking out his dirty head from the creaking grill, Marco carefully assessed his decision as he looked at me and the spread out treats.

My first impression was not very positive as he was an incredible filthy gray color which included enormous black spots on his back. Joy explained that Marco found a small container of hamburger grease on the grill and greedily slurped it down. As Joy tried to extricate him from the dish, he had fallen inside, hence the black greasy spotted fur. He eyed the kitty food trail, and watched us both like a hawk, but I was smitten when he looked up at me with beautiful emerald eyes. As we conversed softly, Marco came out and gobbled up each little morsel and inched closer to Joy. Then the most incredible thing happened, he began to rub his greasy fur on Joy's jean leg. Then as she sat cross legged Indian style on the cement, he hopped in her lap. For another hour the behavior continued as she attempted to scratch behind his ear. Quietly, I suggested to Joy, "I think you can pick him up." At first, she shook her head no, but then on the spur of the moment, she decided to give it a try. Marco quickly squirmed down and out of reach, but a minute later was rubbing against Joy's leg, again hopping in and out of her lap. This time when she picked him up, he didn't squirm away but began to purr with the loudest motor sound imaginable.

From that moment on Joy was able to handle Marco. He was turning into an extremely grateful cuddle machine. Poor Marco was forever scratching and tormented from all the flea bites. What ordeal awaited Joy if she tried to bathe him and apply flea medicine to his neck? Would this tiny cute little kitten turn into a mad ball of fur that kicked, scratched and tore her to pieces? The fateful day arrived for Marco to get cleaned. I dropped off an old green wash tub that was not too deep, while Joy prepared for the worst, as she set out towels and put on a pair of old ripped jeans. I asked her if she needed me to drop by to help handle him, but she thought too many people would make him more nervous. Carefully and slowly Joy put Marco's two front paws in the sudsy warm, water, and another amazing monumental event occurred in his young life. He squirmed very little as the warm bath water turned from clear to dark brown. A light tan with blond stripes Marco emerged dripping wet. Joy toweled him dry and found his fur to be sleek and silky. His patience knew no bounds as he sat and allowed Joy to dab him the back of his neck with flea medicine. Marco was clean, cuddly and almost ready to meet strangers.

A couple of weeks flew passed and as his trust with our family grew, he shyly even began to welcome newcomers into the house and into his life. He was always quick to turn on and rev his motor at full purr. In fact, Marco actually loved to be handled, petted, snuggled and hugged. Each time Joy approached Marco, he seemed to be eternally grateful and thankful for her saving patience and grace towards him. Eventually Marco was adopted by a friend's mom who had recently lost her older cat. She said that she has a permanent, living, furry, blond necklace, because the moment she sat down he crawled up and perched himself around her neck. Marco has become the most affectionate animal she has ever owned. The story of Marco's socialization should be the example and the experience of every new Christian who is found by the Lord and then connected to a healthy church family. As the days and weeks pass, they should lose their wildness and with love and patience from the saints around them, help them to trust and grow into a healthy contributing member of the church. They should not only be influenced by the believers, but the group should benefit as they discover the wonderful plan and purpose that God has for their lives. Healthy relationships within the church family of believers are critical for new believers to become 'tamed and civilized' instead of wild and distrustful.

He who walks with the wise, will become wise but the companion of fools will suffer harm. Proverbs 13:20. (ESV)

Hopefully we will become like the people we hang around with, and like Marco our wild survival lifestyles along with our greasy spots and fleas that threaten to suck out our life's blood, will also be dealt with and removed. That is why it is so important to carefully select who you stay connected with and accountable to. We need the right connections if we expect to move forward and grow in our Christian faith. As the saying goes there is safety in numbers. With the help of the Holy Spirit and God's angelic messengers, the enemy's hold on us can be penetrated, defeated and broken as we are set free from patterns of thinking that have entrapped us. As the old saying goes, if you want to know the character of an individual, look at his/her friends.

Characteristics of a Healthy Church Community

So how do we identify a healthy church community? Think about the story of Marco the kitten as a story about the church community. Through patience, love and compassion we are called to rescue the "least of these," from a life absorbed with self, filth, sin and death to a faith life filled with purpose. Even after Marco's rescue Joy had a lot more work to do. We also need to keep in mind that nothing can be accomplished without guidance and direction from the Holy Spirit.

Echoing this sentiment Dr. Neil Anderson's book, *Helping Others Find Freedom in Christ* suggests that the church's role must be to provide a loving environment so members can find a graceful, supportive and uplifting hand that aids them when their spiritual road hits life's potholes. Dr. Anderson also suggests that Christians should not be quick to judge each other but allow Christ to use them as reconcilers and share the good news with humility, mercy and gracefulness.

In the same way count yourself dead to sin but alive to God in Christ Jesus. Therefore do not let sin reign in your mortal bodies so that you obey its evil desires. Do not offer any part of yourself to sin as instruments of wickedness but rather offer yourselves to God as those who have been brought back from death to life and offer the parts of your body to him as instruments of righteousness. For sin shall no longer be your master, because you are not under law, but under grace. Romans 6:11-14. (NIV)

Sometimes individuals in the Bible had what is referred to as a divided heart, i.e. they serve God on one hand, but are still trapped by the devil in an area of their life. Hopefully in time and with love and correction, they will stop sitting on that fence and quit procrastinating, so they can move forward in their Christian walk.

Scripture:

1. "For I know the plans that I have for you," declares the Lord, "plans to prosper and not harm you, plans to give you a hope and a future." Jeremiah 29:11. (NIV)

2. Strengthened with all might, according to his glorious power unto all patience with and long suffering with joyfulness. Colossians 1:11. (KJV)

Questions:

1. What are some characteristics of a healthy church?

2. Why is it important to stay connected to a local church body?

3. What is the purpose of the local church?

4. Why didn't Marco immediately respond positively to Joy's overtures to help him?

5. What role should the church play in "taming" new converts?

Action Plan

Think about the gifts and talents God has given you. Are you using them in your local church body? If not make a plan to do so.

Confessions/Declaration:

I will keep my appointment with my God given destiny by cooperating with the church community that God has ordained for my training. I will allow and lean on the Holy Spirit to get me through the refining process and allow it to continue to completion even though it seems to be difficult to endure and evades my understanding of how this can possibly take me to my destiny. I will ask, seek and knock at God's door with tenacity and patience, but will not take apart the door to prematurely get there and short circuit his timing, even though I am tempted to do so. I will not allow myself to birth an Ishmael when it is Isaac I am waiting for. I will involve myself as a contributing member and strengthen and be accountable to the local community of believers.

Chapter Notes

CHAPTER SIX

Renewing the Mind, Restoring the Soul

Recently, my husband and I had a problem with wild life in our backyard eating the immature fruit off of our citrus trees. Our solution involved Rick draping some dark, nearly invisible protective mesh netting over the small fruit trees. One day while checking on one of the trees, I noticed a black string wiggling in the mesh. A snake! After my heart quit pounding, I realized it was just a small harmless black racer that got tangled in the mesh while probably chasing a chameleon. Rick tried to extricate the snake by encouraging it to go backward, but it insisted on moving forward, becoming more tangled and finally tried to bite Rick.

Ordinarily, we would have walked away, but I was concerned about my fruit tree. What if this was a female pregnant snake? The last thing I needed was a lot of little snakes wiggling around in my yard. Clearly, we needed to take a different approach. So we (mostly Rick) carefully unwrapped and cut away the mesh with wire cutters while the snake pathetically hung from the mesh. After an hour of snipping and pulling, we got most of the mesh removed and carried the snake to the back preserve while he hung listless, dangling from the shovel. Whether the snake appreciated the help or not I can't say, but I know without our help the snake would have become buzzard bait.

Sometimes emotions get us all tangled up like that poor snake and we seem unable to free ourselves. We are left hanging on to a hopeless situation, like bait, waiting to become someone's lunch. Our brains tell us this in a bad situation, but the emotions have been pricked to the extent that the rational part of us is no longer in control. Despite our better judgment, rather than moving backwards and retreating, we are fearful, headstrong and continue to press into the tangled mess. At some point, despite our investment and losses, we just have to walk away.

There are many self-help authors that attempt to address enslaved emotions. Joyce Myers has written numerous books that talk about how to take control of the mind and capture thoughts and vain imaginations or emotions that try to exalt themselves against the knowledge of God. If you have tried to walk away but are struggling then keep reading and keep pressing into God for answers. We must understand that it is possible to replace our negative or sinful thoughts with positive and correct ones from the Word of God. We have to be willing to take the time and put in the effort to make changes. Experts tell us that thinking is connected to feelings, and a person cannot think two things at once. So a person has to devise a way to put right thoughts in the brain. One of the ways I have done this is to put a scripture verse taped to my mirror along with the situation (or person) I am struggling with. Then I confess aloud daily what God has said about that situation rather than how I feel. When that situation or person comes to mind, the scripture I have memorized pops up. With time and discipline my thought life is no longer being ruled by the negative feeling, the negative thought has been directed to the rear of my mind and replaced by a positive one.

When individuals are emotionally wounded due to circumstances, renewal and restoration, they may require counseling. We have already talked about how the spirit is regenerated through the new birth experience in a split second after confession. This is called *Justification*. The next step is to renew the soulish part of a person that they may live a righteous life which is called *Sanctification*. Psalm 23 states that He (the Lord) restores my soul and leads me in the path of righteousness for His name sake. To become a spiritually mature and healthy disciple of Christ Jesus, a person must yield to the Holy Spirit's inner promptings by dying to deviant outer soulish and carnal desires that war against our higher calling. The Bible tells us that we are made up of three distinct parts: a spirit, a body and a soul. The soul consists of the mind, heart and emotions. Unger's Bible Dictionary defines the soul as the part of a person's personality whose mind, heart, affections and emotions, determine decisions and actions.

He restores my soul; He leads me in paths of righteousness
for His name sake. Ps. 23:3. (English Standard)

In the parable of the ten virgins found in Matthew 25, the five foolish virgins took their lamps but did not take enough oil. Meanwhile the five wise virgins trimmed their lamps and filled them with plenty of oil. As the night drag on all ten virgins fell asleep but suddenly the bridegroom showed up. The five foolish virgins begged the five wise virgins to share some of their oil but they would not. So the foolish virgins had to return to the merchants to purchase more oil. By the time the foolish virgins returned, the wedding feast door was closed and they could not go in. Jesus ending the story saying, "Therefore, keep watch and be ready because you do not know the day or the hour of My return."

Even though all the virgins fell asleep while waiting, it wasn't deemed appropriate to divide the resources of oil. In the story God represents the merchant who is willing to supply to you what is needed for the journey. Oil for the journey represents the soul being daily replenished by His Spirit. A relationship with the Holy Spirit cannot be "borrowed," because each individual must read, study, pray and meditate themselves. God wants to give each of us daily grace for whatever we might face that day, which is why the Lord's prayer is so important.

Our Father which art in heaven, hallowed be Thy name. Thy kingdom come Thy will be done in earth, as it is in heaven. Give us this day our daily bread. And forgive us our debts, as we forgive our debtors. And lead us not into temptation, but deliver us from evil. For Thine is the kingdom and power, and the glory forever and ever. Amen. Matthew 6: 9 – 13. (KJV)

A person must renew all parts of the soul through communication with their Heavenly Father. If the soul is unable to connect to the goodness of the Father because of their wounded humanity then further restoration is necessary. Give Father God all the puzzle pieces of your life and let Him patiently, gently and lovingly in His time put everything back together to the original picture that He had in mind when He created you.

For wisdom will enter your heart and knowledge will be pleasant to the soul. Proverbs 2:10. (NIV)

Renewing the Mind

In *Out of the Belly of the Whale*, I addressed renewing the mind by reading, verbalizing, declaring and confessing God's word. Think of the two year old child who learns to talk by parroting their parent's words. Although the child may not understand the meaning behind the words, imitating is an important first step in the talking process. By verbally conveying information instead of grunting, groaning and crying they make their desires known. Soon the child learns to say words. They may express a strong opinion, but the wise parent knows that the child still does not have a complete understanding about the topic. How foolish would it be to let a child eat all the candy or ice cream they wanted just because they could ask for it? That would not be healthy for them because of their limited understanding of what nutrition their little brains and bodies need for proper development. At that point simply stringing words together that seem to make sense did not justify answering the demand, other things had to be taken into consideration out of the child's purview.

So the novice Christian begins by having a consistent Bible study time. Then Bible passages can be written out that apply to their circumstances. The next discipline should involve verbalizing and declaring God's word then meditating and even memorizing passages. Think of the cow with its six stomachs that chews the grass again and again and then regurgitate the grass to extract every bit of nutrition from it. So we have to 'chew' on scripture to comprehend the implications and prayerfully ask God to help us appropriate the principles identified for a stable, successful and mature Christian walk. This is how to become grounded in our new identity of what God says about you.

> And be renewed in the spirit of your mind; and put on the new man who after God is created in righteousness and true holiness. Ephesians 4:23, 24. (KJV)

> And be not conformed to this world; but be ye transformed by the renewing of your mind, that ye may prove what is that good and acceptable and the perfect will of God. Romans 12:2. (KJV)

My three year old grandson Obed has really grown in his language development. He no longer just repeats words that he has heard from his dad and mom but is now able to understand the meaning behind the words. He puts his words together in sentences to request something he wants to eat or a toy he would like to play with. He is also quick to declare what he possesses by saying, "this is my truck" or "this is my book." When the novice Christian begins to study and memorize God's word or "hides the word in their heart" they may begin by repeating God's word saying this is mine and that is mine but as their mind begins to understand, they learn to obey appropriate heavenly principles, meeting the necessary conditions along with declaring promises and blessings over their lives. As they mature and align with Godly principles, they begin to experience God's abundant life. They must also act responsibly instead of just demanding that God answers their every whim and find out what God wants specifically for their lives. Obed has good parents and they provide everything necessary for his well-being and growth. So also is God a good father who may answer requests quickly or delay or even deny answers to develop faith, perseverance and character. He may have something better in mind. Faith, like mushrooms often develops in dark situations. As the believer learns to love what God loves and hate what God hates, the believer may ask for guidance according to His will.

Thy word have I hid in my heart, that I might not sin against you. Psalms.119:11. (KJV)

Blessed is the man that walks not in the counsel of the wicked nor stands in the way of sinners, not sits in the seat of the scoffers. But his delight is in the law of the Lord and on his law he meditates day and night. Psalm 1:1, 2. (ESV)

Modern Heroes of Faith: Watchman Nee

Watchman Nee was a Christian pastor and teacher who worked tirelessly, wrote and founded over 400 local Chinese churches during the 20th century. Because of the Chinese government's ongoing anti-religion stance Chinese Christians had to meet in secret. Some figures estimate that Chinese Christians numbered about 4 million in the early 1900, when Nee began his church movement. During that time the Chinese government not only persecuted the Christian church but expelled and killed numerous foreign missionaries as well. Today Chinese church numbers may range anywhere from 20 million government registered

Christians to more than 200 million underground Christians. This is a significant number considering the Communist Chinese government under the brutal dictatorship of Chairman Mao Zedong tried to stamp out the Christian church by persecuting, imprisoning and executing many Chinese Christians. Some estimate that this mass murderer killed as many as 45 million Chinese although the exact number of how many he killed, worked, starved or tortured is unknown.

> "The spirit is the noblest part of man because it communes
> with God and occupies the innermost area of our being."
> Watchman Nee

When persecution hit the church in the 1950's, Watchman Nee was falsely accused, tortured and finally imprisoned by the Chinese communist government for the last twenty years of his life, visited only by his wife, probably to keep his church friends safe and from experiencing a similar fate. He died in prison in 1972 and in obscurity or so the government thought.

Pastor Nee preached on numerous subjects including how to overcome the flesh and witness for Christ. Nee began his ministry by publishing books and a Christian magazine. Later his conference notes were hand copied by students and eventually found their way into the numerous books that were translated into the languages of many nations of the world. As a young college student I befriended an MIT engineering student from China, who upon graduation decided to attend a local seminary. Blessing Ng (I changed her name to protect her identity) introduced me to Watchman Nee's teachings through some of his most popular books: *Sit, Walk and Stand*, *The Normal Christian Life*, and *Spiritual Authority*. Pastor Nee never knew the impact his life had, but it created a small wave that crossed nations and become a tsunami to the nations of the earth. Only God can make things like that happen.

According to Pastor Watchman Nee, the mind suffers continual onslaughts of fiery darts from the powers of darkness more than any other part of man. Indeed all temptations offered to man are in the form of thoughts. We must learn how to guard our thoughts from the enemy and the power of darkness, as the mind is the battleground where evil spirits clash with God. Remember Eve was deceived by the serpent's cunning voice that lied about what God had said. A person's mind can become an access road for the enemy to travel upon. We must learn to repulse the evil spirits that war against the simplicity and pure devotion in our minds.

"A person's mind can become an access road for the enemy to travel upon. When this happens we can and will be captive and deceived into losing the sovereignty of our own will." Watchman Nee

Emotions in the Carnal Christian Life

One of our favorite and iconic western movies is *Stagecoach* featuring John Wayne. A memorable scene involves him attempting to grab the reigns of six coach horses barreling out of control to save the maiden in distress. Think of unchecked carnal emotions as those horses. They can derail any God, given vision and send the owner cascading out of control and over the proverbial cliff. That does not mean that all our emotions are bad. After all, God made emotions. When our emotions are healthy, yielded and "riding shotgun," they help to spice up this journey we call life. We wouldn't want to go through life like Spock on *Star Trek* bereft of emotions. So much joy in our lives would be missed. Practically speaking, the goal for all believers is to yield to God by letting the inner spirit control their soul, emotions and body. Being sanctified means the mind is renewed daily while the fleshly and carnal emotions are overcome. We must think with a renewed mind before we act. In short, our identity must align with what God has said about us while resisting the voice of the enemy of our soul.

> So I say then, walk by the Spirit and you will no longer gratify the desires of the flesh. Galatians 5:16. (NIV)

> "The power of the soul is the most substantial, since the spirit and body are merged there and make it the site of man's personality and influence." Watchman Nee

According to Pastor Nee, the more a believer probes into the workings of the emotional life the more he or she will be convinced of its vacillation and undependability. Such a person is controlled by feelings rather than the spirit and is considered a carnal Christian. Nee also stated that many Christians cannot distinguish between emotion and inspiration. Emotion enters the man from the outside i.e. when he considers something like a beautiful sunset but inspiration originates from the Holy Spirit in the man's spirit by inner promptings. Walking after the Spirit means we are governed by principles and laws not by feelings which are subject to change. Often Christians think, "If my feelings agree with the principle then I will do it, but if my feelings do not agree then I will reject it." One example of people being guided by their emotions is charitable giving, which does align with Christian principles, but giving should be guided by the Spirit. Sometimes groups try to raise money by pricking the emotions of the audience. They will show sad pictures of sad puppies and neglected kittens. Obviously, any kind-hearted Christian should be compelled to give, right? But Christians must be wary of allowing emotional responses to replace spiritual guidance. Emotion can also deceive the mind and deny the conscience. Read the following verse. Does your intellect agree but do you still feel condemned in your emotions? If so then you may need to have your soul renewed.

> There is therefore now no condemnation to those who are in Christ Jesus, who walk not after the flesh but after the spirit. Romans 8:1. (ESV)

A Significant Problem Lurking Beneath the Surface

Watchman Nee wrote that the believer's (unregenerate) emotions are the most dangerous enemy that the Christian faces. Pastor Nee said that believers need to get a revelation of what it means to die to their own selfish desires and live in God's abundance. We need to see ourselves on the cross with Jesus, daily. When Jesus died for us, our fleshly controlled emotions died on the cross. Likewise when Jesus was raised from the dead, our emotions were raised to life in Christ Jesus. Many of us are trying to bring back to life what should be dead. The problem with a living sacrifice is that it keeps crawling off the altar. So it is with the Christian who relies on emotions rather than obedience to direct their spiritual walk.

"Actually the soul is the pivot of the entire being, because man's volition belongs to it. How dangerous a master, human emotion is." Watchman Nee

I have been crucified with Christ; it is no longer I who live, but Christ lives in me; and the life which I now live in the flesh I live by faith in the Son of God, who loved me and gave Himself up for me." Galatians 5:21. (NAS)

My husband and I live in Florida where beautiful ponds and swampy areas make an amazing backdrop for the wild life. One of the marshy areas near our house periodically contains hatched baby gators. We like to watch them paddling around the pond, catching insects or sunning in the mud flats. Trust me when I say that all of God's babies are cute, and baby gators are no exception.

As expected, when anyone gets close to the edge of the pond, the babies scurry back into the pond. Not always evident from below the black water is an enormous head that may emerge belonging to the mother gator. She's there to convey a polite message, "Ok, you see them, just so you know, I am here watching, don't get any closer, and isn't it time for you to move along?" When her babies call with a little guttural sucking noise, out of murky black swamp a huge head will emerge. Remember, just like that gator momma is attentive to her babies, God is also actively watching over you, helping with power, wisdom and strength to confront and overcome any problem that threatens us. That is why we must go to God daily, die daily to our fleshly emotions and take on the fruit of the Spirit, and activate His power.

> "You cannot teach a demon or cast out the flesh. You must bind and cast out the enemy and die to your flesh." Pastor Jack Hayford

> Watch over you heart with all diligence, for from it springs the issues of life. Proverbs. 4:23. (NAS)

Hero of Faith, Heart for God: Eric Liddel

After reading about Watchman Nee's influence and legacy in China, I came upon another man who had a profound influence in China as a missionary in the early 1900's. Eric Liddell, a Scottish athlete, was supposedly the fastest man in the world. He won Olympic Gold in the men's 400 meter race in 1924. Liddell's Olympic achievements were depicted in the Oscar winning 1981 film called *Chariots of Fire*. The film compared and contrasted the motivation of two English athletes, Harold Abrahams, a Jew who ran to overcome prejudice, and Eric Liddell, a Christian who ran for the glory of God. When the event date for the 100 meter race was changed to Sunday, Liddell refused to run the event even under the most intense pressure and criticism.

> We have different gifts, according to the grace given us. Romans 12:6. (NIV)

An athlete who heard of the intense pressure Liddell was under, decided to opt out of the 400 meter event that was held during the week and let Eric run in it instead even though it wasn't Eric's best event and he was not expected to win. He honored God with his decision and before his event, he was handed a note by American runner Jackson Sholz which read, "It says in the Old Book, that He that honors Me, I will honor." The scripture was from I Samuel 2:30. Eric did win the event and won the Olympic gold medal. He died during World War II in a Japanese civilian internment camp. He could have been released, but he refused to leave his students, who were also in the internment camp. A new generation of individuals learned about Eric's convictions as they watched the film *Chariots of Fire.* Think about all the athletes and Chinese students who witnessed his conviction first hand, as he refused to abandon them to the approaching Japanese army. In the end, which legacy endured?

For those who honor Me, I will honor. I Samuel 2:30. (NKJV)

Blessed are the dead who die in the Lord from now on. "Yes" says the Spirit, "that they may rest from their labors; and their works follow them. Revelation 14:13. (NKJV)

Renewing the Heart

According to Cruden's Concordance, the word heart used in scripture conveys the seat of life, the center or innermost part of a person and is sometimes interchangeably used with the word mind plus emotions and affections. Just as the physical heart is the principal internal organ that causes blood to circulate through out your body, so the spiritual heart is the part of the soul that uses past experiences and knowledge to determine what emotions we feel and what decisions we make.

For example, a person may experience a debilitating fear of test-taking from grade school that is keeping them from that successful job because they can't seem to pass the next series of tests. When a person's life is regenerated through scripture study, they can ask God to give them a renewed heart that old fears may pass away. This may take some time to occur as they study appropriate scriptures and spend time in the presence of God trading His peace for past trauma and anxiety. It is also a good idea to study for the test! Then they are able to take the test with confidence knowing when they did their part, God was able to do His part by granting peace allowing them to take the test with a clear mind and confidence knowing they will be successful toward reaching their goal.

The good news is that through the process of renewal and freedom, bad habits and insecure patterns of thinking can slowly be changed to good ones. Lifestyle changes can be an arduous process which takes a lifetime of daily accountability and intentional Christian living. It is so important to attend a healthy church and be committed to a good Bible study group or participate in an overcomer support group. Think of how important meetings are for people with alcohol or weight problems. Our heart needs to be a place where God dwells, reigns and directs the course of our lives. We should be careful to protect our heart from wrong companions, influences, and thoughts. We must choose good companions and positive influences. You can't expect to stop a chocolate habit by visiting the candy store daily. What you choose to put before your eyes will determine how successful you will be. Thoughts become words, words translate into actions, and actions become lifestyles, just as being accountable to working out with friends in a gym may help you more than just buying some equipment in your home that ends up gathering dust in a bedroom.

Being Persistent Because You are Loved

My Uncle George used to have a sticker on his old blue Chevy that said, "Keep on trucking with Jesus." It may take several seasons of healing, but be patient with the process and keep plodding along with God's promises. Even an upside - down life will eventually come right side up. If you have gotten lost in the woods, it is going to take time for God to help you get out of them. Continue to abide in Him and let Him abide in you and slowly things that seemed to snare and entrap you in the past, no longer will. Remember to break any habit or wrong pattern of thinking requires bravery to confront and then prayer to take the first step to recovery, then the second and third until you are walking away from your messed up past and into your hopeful future.

All of us are wounded because of the Adam and Eve's fall and require the active intervention of a perfect Creator God's love to fix us. After Adam and Eve sinned, they tried to cover up and solve their problem independent of God. Then they hid behind the bushes. Today, men and woman are trying to figure out how to fix their cancerous sin situations with fig leaves. It didn't work with Adam and Eve, and it won't work for humanity today. It is God alone who can bring amends to the troubled areas of our lives. God offered the price of an innocent animal whose sacrifice and death temporarily atoned for sin and whose skins clothed a naked Adam and Eve. So Jesus Christ's innocent blood is an atonement for our sin and His resurrection from the grave assures us of healing and resurrection for the broken areas of our lives if we are willing to take the journey of healing and partner with Him one day at a time.

Max Lucado wrote a wonderful story called *You are Special* about the Wemmicks who ran around all day giving out gold star stickers or grey dots respectively to those they liked or those they didn't like for a variety of reasons. A certain puppet named Punchinello lived in the village, but unfortunately had been given so many grey dots that who he was couldn't be seen anymore. Finally, he was so depressed he decided to go on an adventure to find the Woodcarver who created him. To his astonishment the Woodcarver had been expecting Punchinello, and was waiting for him to come and be loved by Him unconditionally. He encouraged Punchinello to spend time with him daily. Each time he left the Woodcarver's house, he noticed that one more of the grey dots fell off.

And so we know and rely on the love God has for us. God is love. Whoever lives in love lives in God, and God is them. I John 4:16. (NIV)

Graham Cooke's sermon on you tube called "Inheritance" is all about how outrageously we are loved by God. The first time I heard his message, I hardly knew how to respond and replayed the message repeatedly so Graham Cooke's words could go deep into my heart. Soon tears were trickling down my cheeks as I realized that I had felt unworthy most of my Christian life. It dawned on me that I was so busy working for God that I forgot to enjoy just getting to know and abide in Him. As I listened, I began to realize just how excited God is about each of his creations.... including me! Knowing your heavenly Father is as excited for you to reach your potential as He is should fill you with confidence to tackle any obstacle.

Your eyes saw my unformed body; all the days ordained for me were written in your book before one of them came to be. Psalms 139:16 (NIV)

"I am the vine you are the branches. Whoever abides in Me and I in him, he will bear much fruit; apart from Me you can do nothing." John 15:5. (ESV)

Scriptures

1. If Christ is in you, though your body is dead because of sin, yet the spirit is alive because of righteousness. But if the Spirit of him who raised Jesus from the dead dwells in you, He who raised Christ Jesus from the dead will also give life to your mortal bodies through His Spirit, who dwells in you. Romans 6:10-11. (NASB)

2. And the very God of peace sanctify you wholly; and I pray God your whole spirit and soul and body be preserved blameless unto the coming of our Lord Jesus Christ. I Thessalonians 5:23. (KJV)

3. For we know brothers and sisters loved by God, that He has chosen you. I Thessalonians 1:4. (NIV)

4. Therefore, there is now no condemnation for those in Christ Jesus. Romans 8:1. (NIV)

Questions

1. What are the three parts that make up humankind, and how do they work?

2. What part of your 'fleshly' body is giving you the hardest time?

3. What strategies have you been given in this chapter to keep your flesh under?

Action Plan: Choose one

1. Listen to Excerpts from the Inheritance Sermon by Graham Cooke (in some, message begins @1:20)

2. Write down a scripture that you will tape up on your bathroom mirror (or some other noticeable place) to confess and daily confront any lie the enemy has plagued you with.

3. Watch *Chariots of Fire* and compare and contrast the motivation and legacy of athletes Harold Abrahams and Eric Liddell. Explain whose legacy will endure longer and explain why.

Confession/Prayer

I will take time to renew my mind daily with the word of God and by prayer, yielding my emotions today to God. I will allow God to work on areas of my mind and heart where relationship with Him or others has been broken. I will not be ruled by unhealthy fleshly habits or ideas about myself that are not aligned with God's word. I take authority over the voice of the enemy in my head and cast down what he has said about me. I will walk in the fruit of the Spirit (Galatians 5:22, 23) which is love, joy, peace, patience, long-suffering, kindness, goodness, faithfulness, gentleness and self-control. Against such things there is no law. With the help of the Holy Spirit, I will walk in the resurrection life that Jesus Christ died to purchase and give me.

Daily Declarations:

Choose 3 or 4 declarations, and put them on a 3 by 5 card to place or tape on your bathroom mirror:

- I am loved
- I am fearfully and wonderfully made
- I am accepted in the beloved
- I belong to the Lord
- I am a royal priesthood, a holy nation, perfect in God's eyes
- I am forgiven by His blood
- I am precious in His sight
- I am joyful
- I am filled with His Spirit
- I am fully committed to God
- He is mine and I am his beloved.

Chapter Notes

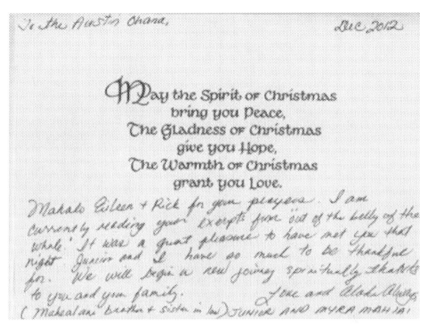

Christmas card from Myra and Junior Mahiai

Family in orange shirts following
Peter and Mahea Austin wedding Dec. 2012

Perter Haik Jacobson
High School Graduation picture 1962

Eileen with Archbishop Desmond Tutu 2003
He left a legacy in South Africa

Irene Jacobson (Mother) – front right
Darlene Kelly (sister) – top center
with Eileen's family from 1995

Joy and Grace 2015

Peter, Grace Andy and Joy
New Year Eve. 2019

Grandma Takouhy and Grandpa John Mangerian
Wedding picture 1911

Andrew and Whitney wedding 2015

CHAPTER SEVEN

HINDRANCES TO MOVING FORWARD

We live in Florida and have become familiar with and respectful of the wild life that occupies the same land and water resources that we do. When walking around a pond or even by the ocean, there is always an awareness that no protective barrier exists between us and the predators like there is at Disney World and Busch Gardens. Vacationing golfers from northern states beware. A seemingly benign alligator paddling around in a beautiful pond is not simply a decorative sculpture to admire. When reaching down to retrieve that stray golf ball landing in the water, they may end up not only losing the ball but a hand or worse. As my mother used to say, "You must keep your wits about you." Christians should keep this truth in mind. Things may not be what they seem and the enemies of our faith are not enclosed in some fenced off area just because we attend church!

Researchers tell us that childhood traumas that have wounded cognitive, emotional and intellectual capabilities can continue to haunt and interfere with a person's ability to have healthy relationships even as adults unless healing occurs. I wanted to title this chapter *Don't Let the Wounded Child of Your Past Drive the Bus of Your Life*. Of course, that title was lifted from someone else's research and would be too long. Still, the truth it declared was remarkable. Tests or trials in our lives may leave a person in the kind of condition that keeps them from fully and properly engaging in life. They seem to be a spectator rather than a participant. In the quiet secret recesses of that wounded person's soul, they have just checked out! Possibly they may be doing just enough "inner work" to keep their issues at bay, so they survive another day. To be healed emotionally, a person must resolve the issues and any inner conflict and that means being willing to do the hard work of rebuilding trust in relationships.

A person's past traumatic relationships with parents or authority figures, when coupled with difficult circumstances, may have violated personal boundaries and created an unhealthy template that has now been branded onto that person's interactions. They think; "This is how I am, what I must do and how I must act to be accepted." As they matured, hurtful incidents from work, broken romantic relationships and other abuse piled on and resulted in additional emotional pain or trauma. Painful events were never addressed because they needed to carry on. When a challenging situation occurred, someone pushed "their buttons" and vulnerable emotions resurfaced causing the person to shut down or careen out of control. They may have to self-medicate these deep and painful emotions by indulging in food, drugs, alcohol or other inappropriate activities so they could handle life. What is strange about this is in seeking relief from their pain they have stepped back into a cycle of repetitive unhealthy behavior. Unknowingly, they are continuing to recreate similar situations to find the acceptance and solutions they never felt. Emotions can be powerful drivers.

But He knows the way that I take; when He has tested me,
I will come forth as gold. Job 23:10. (NIV)

Pastor Janice Russo started one of her messages with a story that illustrated this point. One day a craftsman headed up the mountain with his cart carrying a load of stones for work. As he climbed up the hill, he grew tired and stopped at a relative's house for a drink. Appreciative of the refreshment, he was asked to take some of their stones up the hill, which he did. The next rest stop on his journey was with a friend who asked him to haul an additional load onto his cart that needed to get up the hill. Finally, you guessed it, a co-worker had a small bundle that she asked to place on top of the pile because "he was already heading up the hill." After all, her additional pile wouldn't inconvenience him too much! Rather than say no to these three, the tired, hot and now angry man struggled to get up the hill. He was unsuccessful, the wagon wouldn't budge. Frustrated he sat down on the side of the road, looked up and blamed God for having a load he was unable to carry never realizing that his original burdens were not the problem!

Sometimes these burdens can trickle down to our children and grandchildren as negative attitudes, overall cynicism and bad habits to help 'cope with life'. The Bible says the sins of the fathers are visited on their children and grandchildren to third and fourth generation; some simply call this an old "family curse" that has reappeared. Fortunately for us, the Lord is kind, merciful and forgiving. He knows how to make wrong things turn out right. For overall healthy living, the power of right thinking is essential. With God's help, we can do this.

> The Lord, the Lord God, compassionate and gracious, slow to anger and abounding in loving kindness and truth; who keeps loving kindness for thousands, who forgives iniquity, transgression and sin; yet He will by no means leave the guilty unpunished, who visits the iniquity of the father's on the children and the children's children to the third and fourth generation. Exodus 34: 6-10. (NAS)

A Case for Inner Healing

Society now recognizes the need to assist soldiers returning from battle zones suffering with Post-Traumatic Stress Disorder (PTSD) in adjusting back to a healthy civilian life. Past chaos of war on the battlefield causes physiological stress that also inflicts pain on loved ones. Family members, unsure of how to cope with the mounting pressure, sometimes feel caught in the middle and end up drawing battles lines, attacking one another as frustration builds and communication breaks down. Dramas like *Macbeth*, *East of Eden* and *Gone with the Wind* are fun to watch as the characters battle each other trying to hurdle each chaotic crisis, but toying with people's emotions in your sphere of influence is best left in the theatre. When the feature film ends, at least you can exit and leave with the comfort of a happy ending. In real life only reconciliation can lead a family to a season of healing and recovery.

What happens when unresolved questions persist? Am I capable of being loved? Can I have a normal loving family relationship? Would I be better off alone and never get involved with anyone again? Unbridled emotions got them into trouble once and they suffered an intense emotional setback and perhaps even despaired of life itself. They have never worked through, grieved or received help in processing loss so they decide not to be vulnerable or hurt again. A person may also become disengaged, isolating themselves, and live a lonely life. Bouncing off people like billiards balls, they are unable to have a lasting, deep or fulfilling relationship. Someone or something is inhibiting their present and compromising their future. Deep insecurities, abuse, or fear of rejection pushed them to enmeshment, enabling or being controlled by another person. Dr. Townsend and Dr. Cloud clarify enmeshment as a relationship with an "unsafe person." Dr. Henry Cloud has written several books about setting essential boundaries in relationships. Think about a property line that determines where one person's personal property ends and the other person's property begins. The idea is to think about what my responsibilities are in this relationship and then release the other person to do the same. The boundaries must be communicated and negotiated. Ask yourself these questions:

- Can I successfully control my feelings, attitudes and choices in this relationship when I feel violated?

- Do I have appropriate consequences at my fingertips when boundary violations occur?

- Does my association with that person include respecting each other's feelings and opinions while partnering to resolve any problems that arise?

Sometimes a third party like a pastor or counselor is needed when two people cannot resolve their problems peacefully. After all, we don't want to get in the habit of just ending relationships when what we need to do is to find ways to produce healthy resolutions to conflict.

Dr. Schachter's Two Factor Theory of Emotions

Emotions are located in the part of the brain that processes feelings. Feelings tend to be general and seem to be activated by our five senses, while emotions are more specifically related to the mind. Prominent social psychologist Stanley Schachter is best known for the *Two Factor Theory of Emotions* that stated, environment plus physiological arousal can trigger feelings. The brain appraises the situation and interprets what specific emotions to give to the feeling: fear, anger, guilt, feeling overwhelmed, rebellion, stubbornness, grief, abandonment, depression, unease, sadness, rejection, disappointment, contentment, love, joy, satisfaction, happiness, trust, anticipation, excitement, surprise, etc.

Example: I am nervous and tense, good looking Johnny is here; therefore, I think I am feeling the emotion of love.

By changing the environment we have a different emotion.

Example: I am nervous and tense, but this time I am driving in a blinding rainstorm and the bridge is high and creaky; therefore, I think I am feeling the emotion of fear.

The brain processed the feeling, assessed what it knew about the environment from past experiences, and then gave the vague feeling a very specific emotion. In both cases the feelings were general and came from the sense of feeling tense or uneasy, but it took the brain to assign the specific emotion. In other words, a person may have the same general feeling, but if they are put in a different environment they may experience a very different emotion. The amazing brain efficiently runs through its database of files and decides which emotion to give to a general feeling. This happens many times in a day as individuals experience a range of feelings and emotions. Usually feelings come and go quickly but emotions in the brain can be longer lasting. Emotions may also be deceiving and give incorrect input like guilt or anxiety, suggesting all kinds of things at any given hour of the day and as many times as we feel something. Therefore, it is very important that we examine our feelings in context of the present situation with an awareness that our past experiences contribute to our present interpretation of our experiences. We must learn to separate our thinking from God's way of thinking by using the template of the Bible as our guide for correct living. Our emotions can lead us down a primrose path to disaster, so don't let unbridled emotions lead you astray.

> Casting down imaginations and everything that exalts itself against the knowledge of God and bringing every thought into captivity to the obedience of Christ. II Corinthians 10:5. (NKJV)

Fruit of the Spirit vs the Flesh

According to Unger's Bible dictionary, the flesh is the sensuous nature of man and separated from Divine influence. Unless they are fully yielded an individual's flesh is prone to sin and opposed to God; warring against, and at times overruling the spirit and soul, especially in weak individuals. That means that when emotions and flesh are in control, a person's better judgement may be overruled even though they know what they should have done in a certain situation.

Those who live according to the flesh have their minds set on what the flesh desires; but those who live in accordance with the Spirit have their minds set on what the Spirit desires. Romans 8:5. (NIV)

How do we distinguish when our thinking should be embraced and when our ideas are harmful and need to be rejected? In the book of Galatians 5: 19 – 25, the Apostle Paul gives us a laundry list that identifies when the flesh is in control and when the Holy Spirit is in control. If you list those negative and positive characteristics side by side, a line could be drawn which identifies the ideal characteristics and then contrast it against the antithesis. For example, instead of sexual immorality, you should have self-control: instead of separating factions, you should have faithfulness and unity: instead of fits of anger, you should have love, kindness and peace of mind: instead of doubt, you should have faith. By daily and consistent God time and prayer and listening to Holy Spirit's direction, the wonderful fruit of the Spirit will begin to manifest and increase in your life. Think of a person hitting a baseball: the more practice they get in, the more chances they have to be successful. With diligence they may even begin to make an occasional home run. As the old saying goes, practice makes perfect. When a person has positive emotional experiences with God through praise and worship and takes the time to study scripture to rewire their brain with positive emotional messages, so their positive thoughts will become dominant over negative ones.

For as he thinks in his heart, so is he. Proverbs 23:7. (NKJV)

Sometimes individuals have low self-esteem from an emotionally bruised past which leaves them feeling a dollar short and a day late. They cannot seem to measure up because they are plagued by feelings of inadequacy and cling to a stronger person for self-worth. Their well-being is based on the needs of that other person. Another human being cannot make you feel adequate and healthy. God's desire is for each person to appreciate the way they were made. God does not make junk. When we know who we are in Christ, then we are able to have a healthy self-image and live in community instead of in isolation with other toxic and unhealthy individuals.

Schachter noted that the brain can also stop emotions from interfering with mental functioning because there is a specific executive processing area that filters impulsive expression. After reading several stories about the Boston Marathon Bombing, and noting first responders and emergency room worker responses, there seems to be veracity to this theory. When the bombing occurred, they attended diligently to the injured despite feelings of horror and emotions of fear. Many lives were saved due to the quick thinking of these workers who said something like this: "I needed to do my job so I ignored my own feelings and got to work and comforted the victims in the best way I could, assuring them that they were now safe."

Some individuals wrongly believe that they cannot override their emotions and make rational decisions when they are in crisis, but that is not true. Those first responders eventually did have to take time to grieve, weep and acknowledge hurt feelings after the initial crisis abated but when they needed their brains and hands to work, they did their job, despite what they saw, felt and experienced. If emotions are out of balance and seem to be out of control due to exhaustion, weariness or grief, then that may not the best time to make a major decision, because the negative feelings may sway the brain's better judgment. Better to wait until the sun rises, and then ask God to help you make decisions based on Biblical principles, good judgment and sound council from those who have your best interest in mind. In that way at the end of your life you will have fulfilled God's purpose and end up living the life you were meant to live with no regrets.

Your eyes saw my unformed body; all the days ordained for me were written in your book before one of them came to be. Psalm 139:16 (NIV)

Unhealthy Dysfunctional Relationships

Broken emotions impact the how and why relationships are formed and that is why we must seek wise council in our horizontal relationships. Beware when someone has crossed the line and begins to interfere or try to put themselves in the place where only God should be and then tries to isolate that person from healthy fellowship with others. Remember any relationship that interferes or comes before God is idolatry no matter how spiritual that person may appear to be. In that case you are not the problem but someone close to you is. In Pat Springle's book *Untangling Relationships, a Christian Perspective on Codependency*, individuals are taught how to recognize and push back from relationships with "control freaks", no matter what shape or size they come in: parent, spouse, partner, boss, friend, co-worker, or even pastor.

Pat Springle's book gives tips on how to recognize and have proper boundaries with their partner and how to recognize an unhealthy love relationship. One danger sign or extreme kind of one up (control) and one down (controlled) relationship is when someone defines love as dominance. They may even threaten the non-dominant or passive individual in the relationship with threats or attempt to inflict guilt or codependence that should act as a red warning flag. When someone says something like this we need to be on our guard:

- If you don't do such and such, then I will leave.
- Where would you be without me?
- I simply cannot live without you. I would die without you.
- Without you my life is empty. You make me whole.
- You define me, when I am not with you I am hopelessly lost.

If the controlled person becomes passive and withdrawn because they don't want conflicts to arise, they tend to let the other person in the relationship to do all the thinking and decision making. The submissive person may be psychologically punished with either emotional withdrawal or manipulation, so the controlling person can get or do what they want. Then there are the spiritual accusers that do the enemy's bidding by quoting Bible verses, using guilt trips or judging to get or keep their victims in a relationship which fits their personal agenda. They use God as an excuse for maintaining control while demanding self-sacrifice to them. A true spiritual person knows when it is time to put down the Bible and do what it says.

The dance of enmeshment takes control to another level. According to Springle this is a toxic dance step where one person is emotionally responsible for the other by always trying to keep that other person happy. This is unhealthy because their energies are spent trying to predict how the other feels and what their needs are. Rather than knowing their own emotions, thoughts, or attitudes, all behaviors are done to please that other individual. When you ask them how they are, they need to check with the other person or maybe the controlling person answers for them.

Example: Parents have good days only when their child (even if they are an adult) has a good day, which means the relationship is codependent. You ask them how they are and the answer depends on how their son or daughter is doing or feeling rather than knowing what they feel. They answer for the other person's feelings rather than their thoughts. They rely on the approval of the other person before allowing themselves to feel happy. You can have support from a caring individual like a parent or spouse while sharing a healthy emotional boundary.

The controlling person may even expect the controlled person to give physically, materially or emotionally while they contribute nothing to the relationship admonishing the other person with Bible scriptures like, "turn the other cheek" or saying, "if you call yourself a Christian, then you should do the following," keeping the controlled person in bondage to the dominant one, while invoking God in order to gain an advantage. When the assertive person has a huge mood swing and gets violent, they expect their partner to forgive automatically and ignore their outbursts and not confront them about their bad behavior. From threatening statements to sincere sounding compliments, the person uses emotional highs and lows, physical violence, emotional bullying or even intimacy to get what they want. In extreme cases, the manipulated person begins to even question their perception of reality, which is referred to as gas lighting. This term was taken from the 1944 movie *Gaslight* in which the husband manipulated the wife to the point where she thought she was losing her mind.

All of these are examples of mistreatment in a relationship where the victim enables their abuser. We owe each other love and forgiveness, but trust must be earned through time and by treating each other properly. When the abuse has gotten so bad that the enabling person feels like a prisoner and unable to break free, then the manipulated person may need the support of a group or safe house until they have enough confidence to break free from the relationship. There are resources and safe spaces available for those escaping domestic violence. Comforting words for the victim are not enough. If you or someone you know is in a relationship like the one I have described, encourage them to get help.

Sometimes in unhealthy relationships the abusive person may manipulate, demand and dominate but are disguised as the helper. Interestingly enough in these kind of relationships the supposed passive person may actually be in control. The aggressive person gravitates to needy people to feel more powerful. In these types of relationships, one is the powerful one while the follower is considered an enabler. One person is letting the other person define their purpose and make all of the decisions. Instead of each having their own distinct identity, the two become indistinct blurring personal boundaries. Fear or insecurity in making any kind of decision without the other person is the overriding problem and that person is going to have to learn how to make good decisions. Eventually, the controlling person resents the one they attempt to control or visa versa. The passive person initially may appear grateful, thinking, "Why should I be angry or frustrated with someone who has done so much for me?" But eventually they tire and want out of the relationship too. If neither one gets help, then this pattern is often repeated in other relationships, over and over again.

Pulling Down Strongholds

One of the best books on the subject of strongholds has been written by Pastor Francis Frangipane called, *The Three Battlegrounds*. Some of the ideas referenced in this chapter come from his book. In the Old Testament, a stronghold was a fortified place that was difficult to assault. Like the cave David hid in when he was running from treacherous King Saul. A negative spiritual stronghold can be a house made of unregenerate thoughts that the enemy defends vigorously through lies. Think of it as an evil pattern of thinking, attitude or opinion about any subject including you, a person in your family or even a situation that never seems to change. God wants to expose that lie to the light of day so change may occur.

Keep in mind that we should live by principles but not formulas. A red caution light should go off when any religious program offers for a price, the key and perfect formula to be healthy, wealthy and wise. In reality this is just another way to keep the law, and earn our own salvation without the benefit of faith in Jesus Christ. The Apostle Paul said that this was why Christ was of no benefit to us. To be healed and maintain emotional balance, Christians must commune with God and the Holy Spirit. When a situation is trying, ask for help to cope. Then faithfully commit your way to the Lord and trust Him to be faithful to bring your dreams and desires to pass in His own time and way. You can never move away from the relationship with Him. That is when you have to exercise another fruit of the spirit: patience. In our instant fast food and drive through lifestyle, Christians may be unhappy at the prospect of having to wait for the manifestation.

> You who are trying to be justified by the law have been alienated from Christ, you have fallen from grace. Galatians 5:4. (NIV)

> "The beginning of anxiety is the end of faith, and the beginning of true faith is the end of anxiety." George Mueller

Think about the scripture that states "Do not let the sun go down on your anger." God acknowledges you may feel angry because of what someone did or didn't do, but you don't have to act out the anger and keep fueling the fire day after day by meditating on how angry that person or situation made you feel. There must be a willingness to deal with the deep-seated anger by allowing God to get to the root of the problem; then you can forgive and release that person. Simply put, you don't have to wait for feelings of forgiveness to surface, but you must be disciplined enough to yield to what God has said about the offended releasing the offender.

Our Christian world view should not be molded by the world's view that is contrary to what God has said about a given topic or situation. For example, sometimes naive and young individuals can be brainwashed by Hollywood movies and the lyrics of songs with regard to "falling in love," rather than regarding what God has said about love, relationships and emotions. Worldly love is identified as a euphoric roller-coaster feeling that causes a person to obsess over another person who makes their spine tingle and legs turn wobbly. Sometimes parents (or grandparents) define love as indulgence. Instead of teaching a child to be disciplined and to control their emotions, the parents constantly give in to the child's tears; temper tantrums and bullying are indulging not loving. If the parent does not bring appropriate correction to the child, they may find that they have not just raised a spoiled and undisciplined child but a child that grows into an unruly and compulsive adult. Misguided emotions in attempt to meet their own needs can be the breeding ground for various addictions.

In contrast, the Bible defines love as an action verb stating that true love means caring for people in practical ways, not just a mushy driven emotion that is here today and gone tomorrow. I Corinthians 13 states that love is patient, kind; it does not envy (demand other people's stuff) does not boast, is not rude, irritable or resentful and does not insist on its own way. Jesus Christ dying on a cross for our sins is an example of the greatest and truest love, and contrasts what the world says love is. Next time you are in the grocery aisle to check out the magazines covers and notice how unsuccessful the world's way is, especially when it comes to love, family and marriage. All you will find is drama and disaster. Bill Johnson, Senior Pastor of Bethel House in Redding, California, says that the enemy of our soul travels upon the roadways of our negative thought life to get access to our hearts. Therefore, we cannot afford to think any thoughts that are in opposition to what the heavenly father thinks about us. If we continue to allow the enemy to control and access us through our thought life then don't be surprised when the enemy captures you and keeps you in his stronghold, bound even against your own will.

> Casting down arguments and every high thing that exalts itself against the knowledge of God; and bringing every thought into captivity to the obedience of Christ. II Corinthians 10:5. (NKJV)

Strongholds: Examples of Specific Emotions Out of Control

Obviously, we are unable to address all the possible emotions that can overwhelm us and be out of control. Worry, fear and guilt are common unchecked emotions that many Christians struggle with and don't seem to overcome, but scripture commands us to quit ringing our hands, worrying about what we did in the past or will do in the future and for goodness sakes, "fear not!" It is worth mentioning that fear may also be attached to the demonic realm. We must also be able to discern thoughts in our mind that come from God and which ones come from our flesh or the enemy. By using the gift of discerning of spirits (I Cor. 12: 7-10) and submitting to the Word of God plus getting council from trustworthy and strong Christians who are familiar with the voice of God, we can prevail in any trial that comes our way. If a "brilliant idea" of ours contradicts God's word or a Christian friend who knows the voice of God has a great reservation, slow down, reconsider and rethink that decision.

Satan may appear as an angel of light but appears to have limited access to the believer for trial, punishment or even the sifting of carnal believers. The good news is that Jesus Christ is our advocate. If we have a strong relationship with Jesus and apply the time tested principles in His word and prayerfully listen to His voice and allow others who have gone through similar trials to speak into your life, you will overcome any trial. It is important to allow the Holy Spirit in us to direct our paths because He is stronger, wiser and knows how to defeat the deceiver and his devices. After all He has been with God the Father from the beginning and knows a thing or two about the enemy and how he works. As King Solomon pointed out, "There is nothing new under the sun."

> Dear Friends, do not believe every spirit, but test the spirits to see whether they are from God, because many false prophets have gone out into the world. John 4:1. (NIV)

Our Adversary the Devil: Resisting the Voice of the Stanger

A certain man had a beautiful teenage daughter that ran away to the big city with a boyfriend. Soon she was broke, lonely and abandoned. Without other options, she decided to call her dad to see if he would have anything to do with her. To her amazement, he was not only happy to hear from her but immediately caught a flight to where she was so he could bring her home. When he found her, he was shocked at how altered her appearance was. She was dirty and thin, her poor diet reflected in the acne that covered her face. He tried to get her to eat more so she could regain her health, but she refused. When he confronted her, she explained that the stranger's voice in her head kept telling her she was too fat. The dad said that she needed to stop listening to the voice that was contrary to the loving voice of her father and she needed to agree with what he was saying about her size. The more she listened to the voice of her father, the quieter the other voice became and eventually she stopped listening to the lying voice of the accuser altogether and internalized the truth her father had told her. From that point on she really began to heal both inside and out. If a voice goes contrary to what God's word tells you about yourself, then it is a lie from the enemy.

It is important to remember that as this young lady moved home, went to church, attended Bible study with her friends, she became conformed to the image of Christ, but she needed to be patient with the process! From time to time, she messed up and had a relapse and forgot her identity. When those times came, she remembered that she never stopped being a daughter to her father. She was loved unconditionally. She rediscovered the purpose and her destiny began to unfold. So it is with you: if you mess up remember to pick yourself up, brush off and begin again. Pastor Graham Cooke says that Christians no longer have a sin problem because it was paid for on the cross, but they may have a bad habit problem that needs to be overcome.

Jesus's death on the cross should always remind us of how much God paid to purchase a relationship with us. Jesus died to redeem us so there should be no more fear, despair, guilt, shame, worry, rejection, depression, anxiety, or low self–esteem issues. We are already winners and should delight in that great love He lavished upon us by Father God moment by moment. Then we can begin to walk in the DNA of our God life as a son or daughter one breath at a time. Life has meaning, bondages are overcome, and shackles are broken, as we enthusiastically embrace our future one day at a time. Kingdom living means leading the life God intended for us all along as though we had never sinned. Being buried with Him in death and emerging daily to live in Him from powerless to powerful from sinful to righteous from a slave to a joint heir is an exciting way to live.

Many years ago, when I was in White Mountains Bible School, as a seminary student, evangelist and founder Clinton White, brought in a large threatening picture of a African lion with gapping open jaws that looked like he was ready to pounce on and devour his prey. This picture is an apt illustration that reminds us that you can only defeat this type of predator with the guidance and help of the Holy Spirit. It is never wise to underestimate such a foe.

> Be sober be vigilant because your adversary the devil
> walks around like a roaring lion, seeking whom he may
> devour. I Peter 5:8. (NKJV)

An adversary, according to the dictionary, is a person or group contending against another. This word also suggests an enemy who fights determinedly, continuously and relentlessly. Picture that lion ripping apart and devouring a baby antelope: this is the idea behind the word. Synonyms for this word include our spiritual enemy Satan, foe, enemy, struggle, devil, and hostile spirit. Consider this the next time you are tempted to fold under a trial. This enemy isn't out to just make you slip and sin, he is out to completely devour you! Satan is called accuser or slanderer of the brethren in Revelation 20:10. There will be a final battle see Rev. 12:7-11 and then the accuser will be hurled into the lake of fire in Revelation 20:10, but until then we must cling to our heavenly Father and actively resist Satan.

After Jesus defeated the enemy, sin and death, at the Cross and rose victorious from the dead, He returned to heaven to the right hand of the heavenly Father God and sat down on the throne that had been prepared for Him. It is always about our relationship with God, therefore we must pray and ask in Jesus' name to know how to specifically defeat and overcome the enemy in any situation and put that particular situation at his footstool. Be assured that it will probably involve listening for and obeying God's voice as we confess His word, apply the blood which calls to mind what was accomplished by the sacrifice by Jesus Christ when He shed His blood on the cross and with the help of the Holy Spirit overcame the flesh.

And they overcame by the blood of the lamb and by the word of their testimony and they loved not their flesh unto the death. Revelation 12:11. (KJV)

The Lord said to my Lord, "Sit thou at my right hand, until I make thine enemies thy footstool." Psalms 110: 1. (KJV)

We are never to partake in the devil's slander of fellow believers, who have also been purchased by the blood of the lamb. Jesus said in John 15 that He did not come to judge the world but to reconcile us back to God. Sometimes a lot of prayer and mercy is required. The battleground in the earth is for men and woman's souls. God will never give up on us, so we must never quit believing for others. This is what it means to fight the good fight of faith. Pray without ceasing, the scripture tell us. You will never win a battle against such an adversary on your own. Therefore, when interceding for others, pray in tongues for wisdom, plead the blood of Jesus over that person and declare the word of God over them!

> Therefore brethren, having boldness to enter the holiest by the blood of Jesus, by a new and living way, which He hath consecrated for us, through the veil, that is to say His flesh. Hebrews 10:19-20. (NKJV)

Pastor Ed Russo of Life Church in Wesley Chapel, FL states that at the foundation of every sin is a lie that must be exposed to be defeated. Demons sometimes protect and attach themselves to a person's own thoughts and doctrines. Once a person is deceived, they cannot recognize the deception because they are deceived! Demons will fight and cloak themselves within a person's very own thought patterns to protect access to their life so they can "have rest." To uncover and dislodge the enemy takes spiritual warfare. When we have areas of our lives that are not conformed to Christ, we must sincerely repent and ask the Holy Spirit in us to strive with these hostile thoughts and not give the enemy rest until we are completely delivered. Do not try to justify why you are doing this. Just repent, turn around and with the help of the Holy Spirit, head in the opposite direction.

Realize the enemy of your soul will try and hinder your progress, but be persistent, recognize what and who you are dealing with, and use the authority God has given you and continue to move ahead and in this way, your righteousness will prevail against evil, even within yourself.

> But he (Jesus) turned and said to Peter, "Get behind me Satan. You are a stumbling block to me." Matthew 16: 23. (NASB)

> We wanted to come to you, I Paul more than once and yet Satan hindered us. I Thessalonians 2:18. (NASB)

True repentance means grieving and being broken-hearted about an area of sin not because you have been caught, but because it offends God and ultimately interferes with your relationship with God. King Saul was sorry that the prophet Samuel caught him disobeying God in offering sacrifice. David's sin with Bathsheba, although seemingly worse, was forgiven because David grieved over his sin and moved from sorrow to repentance when he was confronted by the prophet Nathan. He knew he had broken God's heart. Because David loved God with all his heart, David's heartfelt repentance prompted deliverance. God concerns were David's priorities so David's dilemmas became God's priorities.

Modern Faith Heroes: Dr. Rosarrio Butterfield & Todd White

Dr. Rosarrio Champagne Butterfield, former professor of English and Woman Studies at Syracuse University, describes herself as an unlikely convert and "train wreck", with this to say regarding unhealthy emotional relationships and why being free from them is so critical. "There is someone on the other side of our disobedience, waiting for our story so they too can be set free." The statement is a strong one. She likens emotional dysfunction to sin. She further states that emotional health requires renouncing or acknowledgement of what is wrong with us. Dr. Rosario Butterfield messages and books are transformational. In other words, own up to your issues; and enter a discipleship or accountability program for ongoing support for a healthy lifestyle so addictions can be overcome by a Christ-centered lifestyle.

Todd White was a drug dealer and violent man who said that he was at the point of suicide and was about to blow his brains out with a gun when he impulsively decided to look up churches in the phone book. After speaking to the pastor on the phone, he visited the church and spoke to him directly. Todd was smart and desperate enough to know he needed help and could not tackle these destructive and demonic thoughts by himself. The pastor listened to Todd and his hopeless tale of woe and gave him some amazing advice: "It seems to me that you are no longer interested in your life, how about giving it to someone who wants it?"

Todd was intrigued and couldn't imagine anyone who would want it. The pastor said, "Jesus Christ."

Todd did what the man suggested and prayed a simple prayer of commitment and became a Christian. Then Todd said to the pastor, "Hey, you're my spiritual dad."

The man replied "No. If I take on the responsibility of being your dad one of these days when you need me, I am not going to be here. God will always be there for you, He is your spiritual Dad."

So Todd began to read the Bible diligently, pray and listened to the voice of the Holy Spirit and became close to the Heavenly Father. With that, radical changes occurred in his life. If you want to hear someone who is committed to Christ, who will challenge and bless you, go to you tube and listen to either Rosario Butterfield or Todd White's testimony.

Balanced Emotions & Healthy Safe Relationships

God's desire is for you to go deep and heal traumatized and painful emotions of the past and reset balance in your life so positive changes can occur. As we read in the last chapter, our thought life drives emotions. Therefore, it is important to be attentive to any loaded emotional triggers or situations that cause a deeply embedded unhealthy emotion to arise and translate into twisted thought patterns. As mentioned before, enmeshment occurs when someone cannot tell the difference between their own emotions and those of the person with whom they have a relationship. There is an overwhelming feeling and need to be rescued from their own emotions or just to mirror the other person's feelings of anxiety or depression concurrently instead of being in touch with how they feel. This is an indicator that an individual does not have healthy boundaries in a relationship. God's design is that each person grow up to the point where they have their own emotional space, identity and feelings. Each of us must make a conscious decision to grow up and become responsible for our choices, decisions and problems.

We must also choose healthy friendships to aid and maintain healing and avoid toxic relationships. According to Dr. Cloud and Dr. Townsend that means having good boundaries and choosing safe relationships. Identifying safe people includes individuals who:

- take responsibility for themselves vs being irresponsible and always finding an excuse or someone else to blame for their problems.

- are not only able to start a relationship but maintain, and stay present in the relationship. They don't "drop off the map" abandon or disappear and contribute to the relationship.

- don't feel the need to be perfect or have every conversation revolve around them, versus someone who never really shares anything deep about what is going on with them. They pretend to be perfect, having a perfect family, job or home. You feel isolated, even after spending time with them because you never really connect with their true self.

- are spiritual not just religious; they go to church, read their Bible but are not judgmental or self-righteous telling you what you need to do. A safe spiritual person doesn't just check all the religious external boxes but are willing to put down their Bibles, roll up their sleeves so to speak and live what the Bible says. They understand true humility, compassion, mercy, etc.

- are trustworthy and do not demand trust but earn it. When they make a mistake, they own up to it. They don't just tell you they are sorry but they actually repent, change and do what is necessary to restore the relationship and help it to be healthy.

Finding the balance between loving submission and control plus loving others and not being walked on just because we are Christians must be our goal. All of this has to do with renewing the soul, mind and heart. We must decide daily to control our various fleshly emotions and yield them to the Lordship of Christ and His Word. Not denying or suppressing them but allowing unhealthy feelings and emotions to surface and vent appropriately while the brain (not your emotions) decides how you will act on a given day. Remember, emotions are thought driven; therefore, if you are not happy about what you are feeling, discipline your mind and choose to think about something positive. You can only think one thought at a time. Begin by memorizing scripture like the little two-year-old who parrots their mom and dad's words. Then take your authority and cast down wicked imaginations. Renewing the mind to God's word is critical otherwise wicked imaginations can control us.

Scripture says we reap what we sow. If you sow to the flesh, you reap destruction. Are you happy with what you are reaping? If not, change what you are sowing. Submit yourself in love to a small and healthy accountability group which will help you to focus and overcome any problem or bad habit. The group must be trustworthy with your information, so you can take the time to renew your mind in a practical time frame. Sometimes bad habits take a while to change. Good Christian friends help to hold you accountable and support you when you fall down too. If the circumstances are extreme than prayerfully seek out a Christian counselor who will not tickle your ears, but speak the truth in love so you can be set free. Some churches have 12 step programs that help to guide you every step of the way. New Hearts and Transformation Ministries are examples of ministries that teach individuals how to "take every thought captive," to conquer those relational hurts and sexual addictive behaviors that prevent individuals from entering into the love of Christ so Jesus can be both Savior and Lord.

In healthy adult relationships, there are no power struggles - just deep connections with trustworthy and sincere people who love each other. Each person in the relationship has their own distinct individual emotions and ideas about life, with clear boundaries, and is able to love and pursue their own dreams and plans that God has laid out for their life and their future.

Scriptural Declarations:

1. Create in me a clean heart oh God and renew a right Spirit within me. Cast me not away from thy presence, and take not thy Holy Spirit from me. Restore unto me, the joy of my salvation, uphold me with thy free spirit. Psalm 51: 10 - 12. (KJV)

2. Because he who doubts is like the wave of the ocean, blown and tossed by the wind. That man should not think he will receive anything from the Lord; he is double minded man, unstable in all his ways. James 1:6 - 8. (NKJV)

Questions:

1. Explain what the difference is between feelings and emotions and how they work?

2. What is an example of a dysfunctional relationship?

3. What is God's design for a healthy relationship?

4. Have you listened to the stranger's voice? Find two scriptures which you can confess daily that reflect a positive outcome in that area.

5. If this area is too difficult to overcome alone, are you ready to humble yourself and find a trustworthy group to be accountable to, to help you maintain freedom?

6. If you are in a dysfunctional relationship, are you ready to begin the journey to become free?

Action Goals

1. Listen to the testimony of Todd White and/or Rosario Butterfield on *You tube.*

2. Listen to and take notes on one presentation from You Tube either by Dr. Cloud or Dr. Townsend: *How to Say No* or *How to Identify Safe People.*

3. Are you ready to renounce and forsake an area of sin, write your decision and put today's date.

4. Research a person or small group that specializes in helping people in this area. Write down the information. Then prayerfully select a date to contact and join the group.

Prayerful Confession

Lord, thank you for helping me be led by your Spirit. I believe that I am in the right place at the right time, doing the right thing. If I am not then I choose to make adjustments prayerfully knowing that everything God has not called me to do will in the end be burned up or judged. God's Spirit bears witness with my spirit that I am a Child of God born of the Spirit and therefore according to scripture that as many as are led by the Spirit of God are the children of God (Romans 8:14). The Spirit of God leads me, by the authoritative voice of the Holy Spirit. Lord, I choose to forsake any unhealthy emotion not under control and ask you to help me make healthy choices and to get my flesh under control. I ask you to lead me to someone today or a program this week that can help me to be free in the area that I am trying to overcome because to continue in that area I know is not the will of God for me.

Please help me not to be afraid to step out and take the first step. Encourage me to be brave, courageous and not discouraged when I mess up and to accept my humanity when I fail. I am determined to pursue God with my whole heart and will follow the Spirit of God, study my Bible, pray in tongues, make right choices and friends. I choose to do everything that I need to do to become healthy and whole. He is rising up big in me, giving courage to my mind and strength to my body, giving direction to my spirit and I am lead by the inward witness and voice of God.

> God grant me Serenity to accept the things I cannot change, the Courage to change the things I can and Wisdom to know the difference. Amen.
>
> Reinhold Niebuhr

Chapter Notes

CHAPTER 8

FORGIVENESS A TRIP WORTH TAKING

Someone once said that bitterness is nothing more than unfulfilled revenge. In his book, *The Count of Monte Cristo*, Alexander Dumas, illustrated this point through the story of the life of a young sailor who chose revenge over forgiveness. In 1815, a young and dashing first mate named Edmond Dantes returned to the port city of Marseilles, France after a long voyage. The ship's captain had died unexpectedly while at sea, and Edmond brought success to the endangered journey by taking command. When Mr. Morrel, the ship owner, discovered the role that Edmond had played in saving the cargo, he planned on rewarding Edmond by making him the new ship's captain, but then a sinister plot unfolded.

Edmond returned to Marseille to continue his life, marry the beautiful Mercedes, provide for his father and take his promotion as ship's captain. Instead he was clapped in irons and convicted of conspiring against the current king and accused of being a Bonapartiste. Three of his friends all played a role in the betrayal, but Dantes had neither knowledge nor understanding of why he had been condemned. Edmond spent years in prison dreaming of the day he would finally exact his revenge. He never noticed how his desire for revenge was making his heart grow cold and his conscious seared. He never thought of the innocent lives that might be ruined as a result of his anger.

Healing Balm of True Forgiveness

True forgiveness is the mental, emotional and the spiritual process of ceasing to feel resentment, indignation or anger against a person for a perceived offense, while refraining from demanding punishment or even retribution. Each person must decide whether or not to forgive and cancel a debt. A true Christian would be wise to follow the example set by Jesus when He forgave all humanity on the cross and did not withhold forgiveness and exact revenge as Edmond Dantes had. The principle is clear; if you want to be forgiven you must forgive others.

Therefore the kingdom of heaven is like a certain king, who wanted to settle accounts with his servants. As he began the settlement, a man who owed him ten thousand bags of gold was brought to him. Since he was not able to pay, the master ordered that he and he wife and children and all that he had be sold to repay the debt. At this the servant fell on his knees before him, "Be patient with me," he begged, "and I will pay back everything." The servant's master took pity on him, canceled the debt and let him go.

But when that servant went out, and found one of his fellow servants who owed him a hundred silver coins. He grabbed him and began to choke him, "Pay back what you owe me," he demanded. His fellow servant fell to his knees and begged him, "Be patient with me, and I will pay you back." But he refused. Instead he went off and had the man thrown into prison until he could repay the dept. When the other servants saw what happened, they were greatly outraged and went and told their master everything that happened. Then the master called the servant in. "You wicked servant, I cancelled all that debt of yours because you begged me to. Shouldn't you have mercy on your fellow servant just as I had on you?" In anger his master turned him over to the jailers to be tortured until he should pay back all he owed. This is how my Heavenly Father will treat each of you unless you forgive your brother from the heart. Matthew 18:23 - 35. (NIV)

Sooner or later each of us finds ourselves in a similar predicament either owing a debt or trying to exact payment from one who cannot pay. Sometimes the debt owed is not financial but emotional. Think of a child raised in a family where there has been drug or alcohol abuse, volatile anger or even excessive control instead of love and nurturing. When the child grows into an adult their "emotional well" may be half full, nearly empty or even poisoned. If you try to withdraw emotion or nurturing from that type of person, think about the "well" they are lowering their bucket into. What do you think will happen when they pull up the contents of the bucket to hand over to you?

The Lack of Forgiveness is Often the Root Cause of Most Emotional Issues

A person who is emotionally unhealthy might not be able to process their normal emotional responses in a useful way. The following chart identifies emotions that have careened from healthy to unhealthy.

Healthy	Unhealthy
anger	unchecked rage
reluctance	withdrawal
sadness	depression
risk - taking	recklessness
fear	panic
guilt	shame
processing	obsession
reflection	anguish

They should find a time to get alone with God. Be honest, trust God to get to the root of the issue, forgive yourself, the person or situation and then let God wrap His arms around you, so you feel loved and restored. Take time to be alone and/ or get a counselor to help work through your emotional issues. I say work, because it is hard work, and there may be pain and tears involved. If this is not done and the true issues are stuffed underground or ignored then these unhealthy patterns are repeated again and again. Individuals may self-medicate and salve these painful emotions with dependency on things like alcohol, food, drugs, angry outbursts, depression or even other unhealthy relationships. This may explain why an abused spouse ends a marriage only to select another abusive mate. None of these are acceptable options. That is why it is necessary to take the time to heal and get in a support group and be sure to do all the sessions. Don't just attend one, so the box can be checked. You want to be healed and restored.

The mantra of our society is, "If it feels good, do it," but let me suggest this to the reader: running solely on unstable "feel good" emotions may seem cool in the heat of the moment, but in the end it is a disastrous and unstable way to live with outcomes that look like more a train wreck with the person carrying a boxcar of regret. Using fleshly emotions and feelings to make important decisions can be like fall leaves that blow in the wind and end up by being crushed underfoot or burned. There is no staying power when the mind and will are not involved in decision making. To prevail, one has to count the costs from beginning to end, be committed to the task, and then prayerfully consider the price to be paid along with a generous sprinkling of wise council from trustworthy people. The Bible gives us some very specific warning signs that believers would do well to consider.

> Get rid of all bitterness, rage, anger, brawling, and slander, along with every form of malice. Be kind and compassionate to one another, forgiving each other, just as in Christ, God has forgiven you. Ephesians 4:31-32. (NIV)

The problem with many Christians is that they do not know enough about their new identity and new nature in Christ. They still believe the enemy's lies about them because of their past, and obsessing about what they did as unbelievers, instead of thinking about what God has said about them as His children. The past in gone, forgiven, thrown into the sea of God's mercy and forgiveness, so put up a sign that says no fishing and discipline yourself to never to visit that place again. The voice of the enemy's condemnation can seem a lot louder and more compelling than the voice of your Heavenly Father. We need to renew our minds to God's word and what God says about who we are and believe the voice of Truth instead of the enemy.

> Therefore if anyone is in Christ, he is a new creation. The old passed away; behold the new things have come! II Corinthians 5:17. (NASB)

Heroes of Faith: My Mom

As the youngest child, I received a lot of affection and attention from my family. Unfortunately as my parent's unstable marriage unraveled, my mom had to focus on keeping her job. Finally, when the home environment became unsafe, the marriage ended with my dad being forced to leave. This placed even more financial pressure on my mom. The ensuing divorce embroiled my parents in a financial tug of war over who would get the home plus other assets. Things got even more desperate when a telegram arrived announcing my brother's death while serving in the navy. Mom was pushed to the edge of an abyss while the home was blanketed with sadness, depression and grief. Most little children are self-absorbed, assuming the world revolves around them and I was no exception. Unable to fully comprehend why the family was in chaos, I only knew that my needs were neglected. Mom's siblings and her mother, my grandmother, tried to provide moral support, but the family home seemed more like a former battleground with walking wounded everywhere!

With the family in survival mode, my two older sisters relied on each other for emotional support as all of us treaded carefully the next couple of years. Schoolwork took a back seat to what was happening at home and as a result, grades in two of my toughest subjects began to plummet. One afternoon, I was called out of class and summoned to a meeting with my high school guidance counselor. He informed me that my prospects for staying in the college preparation course track looked dim because of my failing math and science grades. He never asked about or took into consideration what might be going on at home. He just assumed I was slacking off and suggested that I set a lower bar by opting out of difficult college courses to become a secretary. Devastated and embarrassed, I left his office. With school out for the day and me not wanting to be questioned or seen by friends, I quickly escaped and headed home via the local park where I could really cry. What the guidance counselor didn't know was that my best friends and I had already decided on a local teacher's college where we would all attend together. As I sat on a swing, trying to make sense of all that had recently transpired in the family, I found myself making a quality decision, although I didn't recognize it as such at the time. Not wanting to bother mom about what had happened at school, I determined that somehow I would pass those tough courses and attend college with my friends as planned. It didn't hurt that they were all smart and enjoyed practicing their teaching skills on me.

Ever wonder why certain people are successful while others are not? I'm not sure I can answer that question for everyone, but for me it was the example my mom lived out before me. She put her nose to the proverbial grindstone, went to work each day despite her emotional pain, and set her course to raise her children and provide a home for them no matter what. She planted and nurtured within me a tap root of tough resolve. Her work ethic and dogged endurance and daily plodding along had a positive effect.

Her passion for life taught me to keep moving forward, reaching and grasping for that next step. I knew we kids were her legacy and validation for her straight-laced lifestyle. Mom struggled to find a good paying job after her divorce, having only obtained a high school education. Then and there she decided that all her girls would have a good education to fall back on. Drilled into my head daily was to rely on no one, make something of yourself, develop your character and keep your morals high. Her passion and singular focus were imprinted on me in those early impressionable, albeit difficult days. We clung to our faith, remembered that we were overcomers and 'survivors' due to our Armenian roots, and always had support from our family no matter what! Those values were etched into my psyche and endure to this day.

The local Methodist minister, Mr. Smith, was a tall, lanky quiet man with watering blue eyes and a soft southern accent who seemed sympathetic to our plight. He took me aside one day after church. Someone must have told him about all the family was going through. He wanted to offer condolences and asked if he could come and visit us. We were very proud and private people, so I told him that he didn't need to bother with us as we were just fine. My sisters and I had closed ranks to protect mom who was vulnerable and unable to handle another person 'prying and meddling' in our personal affairs. I suggested that if he really wanted to help me he could tutor me because I was failing in math but all he said to me was, "I am not a tutor." He probably meant well but the assistance he offered seem useless and impractical to my middle school mind. From that day on, I had little use for him. From time to time I would receive correspondence or postcards from him. I know he was praying for us, especially me!

My mom was my example and she never took time off to grieve; she just trudged along and carried all those gapping painful wounds within her soul, working hard each day to provide food and shelter for her children. She never went on welfare or took assistance in any form except from her immediate family as she provided for us the best she could. She wasn't stoic either; she did grieve, often displaying irrational or explosive anger with me at little things that happened and then would go to the other extreme and weep at an unguarded moment. I knew the fragile emotional state of Mom and consequently kept my teenage explosive confrontation and challenges to a minimum or so I thought. I couldn't push too much; she was already teetering towards the irrational edge.

As a family, we never discussed the tragedy or acknowledged the pain, and my brother's name quietly retreated into the shadows whispered occasionally by my sisters and other relatives. As an intense sadness settled like a cloak over our household, it seemed like a long time passed before I saw my mother relax, smile or even laugh again. We acted with as much bravado as possible to the outside world, but inside I was strangely detached, distrusting and anxious about what tomorrow might bring. An iron door slammed shut on my childhood innocence, as the family patched life together and moved on. Humpty Dumpty had cracked and there was no putting him back together again.

Mom knew I loved history and was intrigued with politics from her brother, my Uncle Dickie. She decided that we needed a good lawyer especially because of her ongoing battles with dad. So I spent a lot of time with her in the lawyer's offices, translating on her behalf and her burgeoning plan seemed to take off. Unable to envision how on earth I could possibly achieve a law degree with my horrible grades, I decided to soldier on and keep these thoughts to myself. Maybe one didn't need math or science after all. I managed to graduate from high school in the upper 10% of my class and was accepted to the college of my choice. Off I went to college and it was with hushed whispers and giggles that one day a couple of my high school friends informed me that the guidance counselor's daughter had to drop out of college to be married. Since everyone seemed to have an easier time applying themselves when it came to grades and testing, it surprised me when I discovered that all of them had chosen to major in either early childhood or elementary education. I had to keep my promise to Mom, so I majored in Political Science and found that I was the only female in all of my classes. Depression over the loss of my brother finally retreated and had taken residence somewhere deep within the core of my soul but every now and then it would surface and rear its ugly head.

Beauty for Ashes

Thirty-six years later, memories of my brother's death seemed to be quietly resting when suddenly they resurfaced and crashed through my well-ordered world like the breached levies of the Mississippi River at flood stage. It was a beautiful fall Sunday morning. Our church was hosting a Veteran's Day celebration but when the colorful flag corps came marching down the aisle playing Anchor's Away. It was as if some underground raging flood in my soul had finally found an opening, been unleashed and broken through. Embarrassed, I left the church building quickly because I couldn't stop weeping. After the service I found Pastor Larry Bozeman, one of the sponsors of the event and he told me his story. As a very young returning Viet Nam Veteran, he was greeted at the airport with signs like "Baby Killer." He spiraled downward into alcoholism until he became a Christian and then made the important decision that if ever he had the opportunity he would act as a healing vessel for his generation of veterans and their families. The support that our current veterans enjoy is in large part because of the abuse, reproach and wanton hostility that was greeted by Pastor Larry's generation of returning Vietnam Veterans. These older veterans decided that it would never happen again to our returning young men and woman in uniform.

In all those years, I had never visited my brother, Peter's grave, but Pastor Larry encouraged me to take a pilgrimage and do so. On a beautiful spring morning, I decided to travel back home and deal with the years of stuffed painful memories. Bright yellow daffodils and fragrant tiny white lilies of the valley greeted me as I passed through the gate of the cemetery to find our family plot. Removing the crinkled map containing directions from my mom to my brother's grave, a wave of purple lilacs greeted me. I slammed the rental car door shut and proceeded to climb over the lavender border, hoping no one was around in case I became unglued. Agitated with the New England spring breezes, dainty American flags planted for Memorial Day weekend help me to identify the decorated veteran graves. I followed Mom's directions and soon found Peter with my dad's grave situated pretty close by.

As I had seen my mom do numerous times when I was little girl on her own dad's grave, I bent down to pull weeds from the plaque as I read it aloud. Soon I was reminiscing with lot of decades of stuff to catch him up on. I thought about all of those Italian submarine sandwiches we shared and plastic soldiers and tiny green plastic tanks that we played with in the dirt between ours and the neighbor's yard. A stray tear trickled down my cheek when I reminded him of his broken promise. "You promised to return, to come home and play soldiers with me again but you never did!" Another warm tear splashed down my face. He never saw me grow up, he never saw me married, and he never met my children. More memories, coming faster now as happier days piled over the sad ones. Like the time when he and my sisters had snuck up our attic to give me a birthday party that included treats, a teenage doll, with a couple of extra outfits for her. Peter's gift had been two pairs of tiny high heels that fit her perfectly. A smile now crossed my face as I reminisced and worked harder on the stubborn weeds. Soon pleasant thoughts crowded out the unhappier ones. One by one, the memories marched on setting themselves like soldiers in perfect order. Like a jeweler, who sets a brilliant diamond in a broach, and then surrounds it by other precious stones. No longer sad, I was proud that my brother had followed his heart and done what he thought was right and I even felt pride at his sacrifice. He was still my hero. It felt good to finally get resolution and peace even though it had taken so many years to do so.

Sometimes we sweep painful memories under the carpet and never deal with them, pretending they never took place. They are festering deep within us, affecting and altering our steps. With each precarious step we take, the stack is threatening to spill over. One of these days, the pile is going to trip you up. Sidestepping pain is never the way; it only insures that we will never get closure on the past. As hard as it is, each of us needs to square our shoulders; face the music and cry maybe even bellow with as many tears as needed over lost dreams. There is nothing wrong with grieving over what will never be. Honestly dealing with this messy business of painful memories in a necessary evil. Then we must ask God to give us peace and as the scripture states and He will give you beauty for ashes.

Many years ago as a middle school student, I handed my Grandmother, Takoughy, an olive green skirt that I was supposed to make from a pattern. I was panicking because the following week our teacher was going to grade us on the finished products. It did not remotely resemble the skirt or girl who modeled the skirt pictured on the front of the envelope. My stitches were so messy and haphazard, the skirt hem was grossly uneven and it was impossible to put on the skirt because I sewed the wrong seams together. What a mess! To my horror grandma didn't fix the skirt but began ripping out all the seams. Then to my great relief she expertly repositioned them and sewed the seams back together, the right way with perfect stitches. After she finished, she had me try on the olive skirt. It fit me perfectly. I was so excited that I twirled around and around. Slowly her eyes twinkled as a big grin crossed the lined face. Her old, wrinkled and nimble hands could fix any mess. That is how it is with God when we place the situation firmly in His hands. Forgive yourself, forgive others and ask God to help you to deal with the pain, and heal your heart so you can resume your life instead of just surviving the tragic ruins.

Getting one seam back in alignment will help all the other run ones run straighter. That is why God often orchestrates events that seem to bring all the unfortunate crud to the surface. It is critical that you allow Him to help you resolve past hurts, grieve appropriately and get proper perspective so the injury is no longer festering and dictating how the journey of your life will play out. Sometimes it feels as though God has to take you down to your foundations where the pain and rot of your soul have occurred. He will not leave you there! He will restore, rebuild and heal your soul. If you are brave enough it is a trip worth taking.

Forgiveness: Turning Point

In my last book *Out of the Belly of the Whale*, the topic of forgiveness is thoroughly dealt with in Chapter 10 called *Broken Vessels*. After being sick from kidney failure and on dialysis for two long years and feeling abandoned by God, one day I blurted out a prayer that ended up being a turning point in my sickness. It took a lot of reflection, prayer and soul searching to write about my experiences. It is my hope is that in reading about my journey, others will reach their destination of inner healing. A festering wound hidden in the soul may actually spill over into the physical body manifesting in sickness. Our fallen human nature that we inherited from our common ancestor Adam likes to hang on to the root of bitterness rather than to forgive as Jesus taught us.

A cheerful heart is good medicine but a broken spirit saps a person's strength. Proverbs 17:22. (NLV)

"And whenever you stand praying, forgive, if you have anything against anyone; so that your Father who is in heaven may forgive you your transgressions." Mark 11:25. (WEB)

Although I didn't know it at the time, I held some deep seated resentment, anger and abandonment issues towards my father. One evening, as was our practice, my husband and I prayed and asked God to give us our healing breakthrough. Suddenly, my husband turned to me and said, "I feel as though you still need to forgive your Dad." My dad and I had restored our broken relationship before his death, but I obeyed my husband and searched my heart to make sure I was right with God as far as my dad was concerned. Unknowingly, my husband had hit the nail on the head. The next evening when I did my daily walk I decided to sit down on a grassy hill overlooking the golf course where I often prayed. Suddenly, it was as though dark thunderclouds had rolled into my spirit and emotions. I found myself overcome with tears and anger. When my parents had divorced, my mother had to work to support our family so she was no longer there when I left for school or when I came home. As an elementary student without a mother to come to, the house seemed gray, cold and empty. I felt abandoned with no one to care for me and to make sure lunches were fixed or dresses were clean and ironed for school.

Contrasting my experience, I remembered a friend at school whose mom was constantly doting over her, fixing her breakfast, carefully putting her curly hair in bows, including a special school snack or picking her up when it was a rained. The constant displays of nurturing and kindness, contrasted the neglect I felt almost too much to bare. In a "Leave it to Beaver" society that epitomized the norm, with a dad working so mom could stay home to care for the family, my home circumstances felt strangely out of step. Remembering those feelings of reproach, loneliness and abandonment washed over and tormented my soul as hot tears streamed down my cheeks. I cried as I felt the "Little Orphan-Annie" of my past resurface. I looked up to heaven and blurted out angry words. "God, why have You cursed me? What did I do to deserve all of this?" I sobbed for a while not knowing how much time had passed. Facing the pond, the sun was quickly sinking into the western sky while splashing a soft pink stain across the horizon. After a while, a wonderful quietness and peace crept into my soul displacing all the anger and bitterness. Then these words came into my spirit.

"Child, do not blame Me for your dad dropping the ball in your life. Each person has the decision and free will to do what they want and unfortunately his choice had consequences on you and your family."

God was right. So many difficult things had come upon our family as a result of my Dad's actions, inaction and poor decisions that clearly were not sanctioned by God. I had often wondered if he cared anything for us. So why had I blamed God all these years for a choice that He was not responsible for? Another idea began to crystalize a question, "God, how many times do people blame You for terrible things that others choose to do?" The responsibility for the welfare of my children rested in my hands. I shuddered, thinking about the horrible consequences my children might suffer due to my selfish decisions. As I walked home that evening another uncomfortable revelation entered my heart. I suddenly felt the weight of my parental role. Children do suffer when parents make bad choices. Since night was creeping on, I began to hurry. My husband and I made daily sacrifices so our children were comfortable in innumerable ways, many of them seemingly inconsequential. I thought about all those parents who were making selfish choices that night that would include them not coming home and oh how those children would suffer like I had.

God had not forgotten any of this and was about to do something so amazing, so wonderful that would more than make up for all my past suffering. God in any life is the great "Equalizer," transforming the past so bad consequences no longer hurt your future. That evening I received a call from my precious pastor friends, Derek and Lorna Howard-Browne, asking if they could come over. Pastor Derek said that they had "something" for me. I wondered what on earth it could be as I greeted Pastors Derek and Lorna with my usual anticipation. The "something" they had, was a message from God. I had not breathed a word to anyone regarding what had transpired on the "grassy knoll" of the golf course so the next few moments with that pair were astonishing.

Pastors Derek and Lorna sat down in our family room. Then Derek began to share what God had placed on his heart. Pastor Derek took me by the hand and looked into my eyes as tears began to stream down his face. In his South African accent, he began to relay to me how much God loved me. As he talked the presence of the Lord filled the family room, and I too began to weep. Derek went on to say that I was not cursed but blessed, and then he laid his hands on my head to pray. He blessed me as a brother in Christ, a priest of God and finally as a father. Finally, I had the blessing that I had longed for my entire life. God sent someone to validate what had transpired earlier. He not only hears our tears but the cries of our hearts beyond even the words. What God gave me was for my family too. Soon my husband, my children and I were weeping as the Holy presence of Almighty God filled the room. We basked in the tingling and electric presence of God. My soul filled with sweetness like liquid honey and oil at the same time. This liquid love seemed to overflow and spill into every hidden, nook and crevice of the barren places of my once hurting soul. Overflowing with divine love, love lifted me and healed my soul. Where there was once anger, hurt, loneliness and rejection there was love and an abundance of peace. Never again would I suffer from the feelings of abandonment or curse that I had felt as a child. The old hymn came to my mind. The love of God how rich and pure how marvelous and strong; it shall forever more endure the saints and angels song.

A void was now filled with the presence and love of God Himself. He gave me so much I actually had an extra measure to share with others. God restored the lonely, empty and reproachful years of being from a single parent home. That is why I say that God is "The Great Equalizer." Regardless of how overwhelmed you are from negative experiences in the childhood or youth, in a single refreshing moment God can water the dustbowl of your soul and make it a garden. Within a couple of months of that experience I was given the gift of life as my sister Leilani volunteered to give me one of her own kidneys and make my life whole again.

Scripture

1. For if you forgive those who sin against you, your heavenly Father will forgive you. But if you refuse to forgive others, your heavenly Father will not forgive you. Matthew 6:14, 15. (NLT)

2. Bear with each other, and forgive one another, if any of you has a grievance against any man, forgive as the Lord forgave you. Colossians 3:13. (NIV)

3. So watch yourselves, if a brother or sister sins against you, rebuke them; and if they repent forgive them. Even if they sin against you seven times in a day, and seven times come back to you saying "I repent" you must forgive them. Luke 17:3 - 4. (NIV)

Questions:

1. What do we do when emotions become unhealthy or unstable?

2. What example from scripture talks about what happens when we withhold forgiveness?

3. Give an example of how the author finally resolved her painful memories of her brother's death and parent's divorce.

Action Plan

Are you ready to be healed from a painful memory by either asking forgiveness or revisiting that painful experience so you can grieve and receive God's healing in your life? If so release the torment and listen to what God has to say so healing can come into your life.

Confession/Prayer:

Lord, I forgive anyone who has sinned against me and believe that you will forgive me as I forgive others. I ask you to bring to mind any person, including myself, and any past actions and mistakes that have been made, so that I might release them into your loving gracious hands. I will not willingly harbor any unforgiveness or desire to exact revenge on anyone but instead choose to forgive them completely. Neither do I choose to hold bitterness against them but release them and myself in the name of Jesus Christ. I ask you to heal any damaged or bruised emotions or memories within me from the past and set them in a peaceful order like jewels so I no longer can be tormented by painful memories from the past. In the precious name of Jesus. Amen.

Short Version: "I am sorry, I was wrong, please forgive me." Francis Frangipane.

Chapter Notes

CHAPTER 9

IMPORTANCE OF BEING BROKEN

Today, we don't hear much preaching about being broken, but in the past this was an important topic for Christians. The term being broken is used by horse trainers to describe a horse that trusts a rider and allows a bit to be placed in its mouth and a saddle on its back so it can be ridden. In *The Release of the Spirit* by Watchman Nee, there is a chapter called, "The Importance of Being Broken." Nee states, "There is no one more beautiful than one who is broken!" Stubbornness and self-love give way to beauty in a person who has been broken by God. One man in the Old Testament stands out as one of the best examples of this because of his transformation from being called Jacob, meaning trickster or supplanter, to Israel, meaning Prince of God. Jacob zealously desired God's blessing because of what it could mean for him personally and professionally as the leader of the family clan. Even in his mother's womb, Jacob strove with his slightly older, twin brother, Esau. Jacob eventually stole his brother's birthright with the help of his mother through trickery and deceit. However, in Jacob's defense, Esau had no regard for it anyway and even "despised his birthright." Still, when Esau discovered that he had been tricked out of the inheritance and now would receive only one-third instead of the double portion he would have received as the eldest, he plotted to kill his brother. Rebekah overheard what her son Esau was planning, so she had Isaac hustle off Jacob to her brother Laban's family in Haran where he would be safe. The unfortunate consequences of Jacob's trickery were not only isolation and grief but also that mother and son would never lay eyes on each other again.

As Jacob traveled back to Uncle Laban and his mother's clan, a lonely 600 mile trek, he must have wondered what their tricky plans had gotten him. That was when the first small crack in his self-sufficiency appeared. Weary from the day's events, he rested his head upon a rock and waited for sleep to come as the shadows grew longer. Finally, night fell and as the stars emerged one by one, rustling noises and strange animal howls nearby filled his heart with fear. Jacob tossed and turned but finally fell asleep, and had this wonderful dream about a ladder that reached to heaven. This was his first encounter with the wonderful, miracle- working God that his father had talked to him about.

> There above it (the ladder) stood the Lord, and He said, "I am the Lord God of your father Abraham and the God of Isaac. I will give you and your descendants the land on which you are lying. Your descendants will be like the dust of the earth, and you will spread out to the west and east, to the north and south. All peoples on earth will be blessed through you and your offspring. I am with you and will watch over you wherever you go, and I will bring you back to this land. I will not leave you until I have done what I have promised." Genesis 28: 13 - 15. (NIV)

When Jacob awoke from his dream, he said, "Surely the Lord is in this place and called the place "Bethel" or Gate of Heaven. Then Jacob requested that God go with him, provide him with food and clothing, and return him safely to his father Isaac's house. In return, Jacob promised God that the Lord would be his God. His first inclination was to make a deal with God and give God a condition on their relationship, but God still kept his promise.

Jacob headed to Haran the next day to seek his destiny but he was about to find in his Uncle Laban someone even craftier than he and his mother put together. As time passed, Jacob's skill in caring for Uncle Laban's flock caused them to flourish. Laban even set wages of a certain portion as the animals multiplied, but this was irksome to Jacob because Laban kept switching the wages depending on which animal was bearing. Despite the challenges with his uncle, the flocks kept multiplying, helping everyone to prosper. Perhaps this prosperity was why Uncle Laban agreed to accept Jacob's marriage proposal to his youngest and most beautiful daughter Rachel who had caught Jacob's eye when he first came to Haran. Sadly, on their wedding night Uncle Laban, true to form, did the unthinkable and tricked Jacob by switching brides. We can only speculate why Jacob failed to notice this. After all, his seven years of hard work were finally paying off and perhaps he figured there was no harm in celebrating more than he ever had before. Surely he could let down his guard just the once. Jacob's nightmare seemed to be just beginning when he awoke the next morning to find Leah with him in bed. Although he may have been furious, it didn't matter. It was too late. Eventually he was able to marry the girl he loved, Rachel, but he had to work another seven years to get her.

Leah and Rachel's jealousy and fighting led to their two maids Bilhah and Zilpah picking up where the sisters left off. Everyone seemed to be competing for Jacob's time and affections causing ongoing friction and drama in the family. Jacob spent more and more time away from home learning his craft with the herds and flocks increasing. He continually prayed for wisdom, and as he matured, God gave him additional dreams, angel encounters and blessed peace that included a well-needed respite from home. Everything Jacob's hands touched led to increase including the two sister-wives and their two handmaidens who produced twelve strong sons and one beautiful daughter.

Meanwhile, the large family clan continued to travel farther and farther looking for good pasture land. Although Jacob seemed to mellow and greet the challenging family circumstances with measured grace, the raucous boys were corrupted by quarreling, bad-blood and the influences of their cousins and Laban's paid workers. They grew from mischievous into unmanageable young men who took matters into their own hands, unwilling to be bullied, and thus created one exasperating situation after another for Jacob. Jacob finally had enough and under God's direction decided to take his family and flocks back home to Canaan when Laban was occupied elsewhere. While they rested outside of Shechem's city (Genesis 34: 1-31), his daughter Dinah decided to shop and explore the city. Her beauty got the unwanted attention of the prince of the city who seduced and raped her. After the marriage proposal had been agreed upon between Jacob and the prince's dad, Hamor, Jacob's sons set out to avenge their sister's rape by treacherously wiping out Shechem's village. All of the men were savagely killed and the women and children were carried off along with their flocks and herds. Everything of value was also taken as spoil. Jacob was horrified by the treacherous actions of his reckless sons, but sadly some of his greatest trials were just beginning.

As Jacob got closer and closer to Canaan, his anxiety grew about meeting Esau again so he decided to send numerous gifts to his brother including 220 goats, 220 sheep, 30 camels, 50 cattle and 30 donkeys. He was hoping all these gifts would pacify his brother's wrath. Then he sent the family and the rest of his possessions across the river while he stayed alone in camp. Jacob knew his strength and wisdom came from being alone with God but during the night he encountered a man with whom he wrestled until daybreak.

> When the man saw that he could not overpower him, he touched the socket of Jacob's hip so that his hip was wrenched as he wrestled with the man.
>
> Then the man said, "Let me go, for it is daybreak." But Jacob replied, "I will not let you go until you bless me."

Then the man asked him. "What is your name?" "Jacob."

Then the man said, "Your name will no longer be Jacob but Israel, because you have struggled with God and with men and have overcome." Genesis 32: 25 - 28. (NIV)

Jacob renamed the place Peniel because he said, "It is the place where I have come face to face with God, and yet my life was spared." He returned home to Canaan and reconciled with Esau. God was about to form His own character in Jacob as God carved out from himself a people from the tribes of men on the Earth. From that night on, Jacob limped, leaning on his staff and on God more than on his own physical prowess and cunning. From this encounter of brokenness emerged less of Jacob and more of God. That night would prove to be a turning point for Jacob as he probably realized that the journey God had him on was more about wrestling with his own fleshly way of doing things.

An additional breaking of Jacob's flesh occurred when he lost the love of his life, Rachel, who died prematurely in childbirth, bearing their youngest son Benjamin. The twelve sons became the twelve patriarchs of the tribes of Israel. With Rachel's passing, her older son, Joseph, became the love of Jacob's life. From here the story shifts and the focus of the story falls no longer on Jacob, but on his young son Joseph, older brother of Benjamin. Joseph begins to eclipse all the tender love and focus of his father as the greatest trial and triumph for Jacob are directly ahead. Jacob had hoped that by leaving Uncle Laban, the raucous behavior and bad external influences of his sons would cease but instead he was about to find out that you reap what you sew.

Therefore, if anyone is in Christ, the new creation has come. The old has gone, the new is here. II Corinthians 5: 17. (NIV)

Someone once said the problem with a living sacrifice is that they keep climbing off the altar. Jacob had come quite a long way from his trickster and usurper days but his character and identity as prince with God had not fully emerged. It would take another shattering heart break to compete the process. This came in the form of the ultimate betrayal from his inner circle of trust, his family. The brother's jealousy of Joseph mushroomed beyond containment, as they hatched a plan to put an end to their father favoring one son over the others. The unruly brothers decided to betray and sell the favorite son of Jacob into slavery to a passing caravan headed to Egypt! Unwilling to let their father in on their evil plans, they agreed to say that Joseph had been torn apart by wild animals. When this news reached their father, they never could have foreseen or imagined how strong, he Jacob would be reduced to despair and never ending grief. Jacob fell on his face broken and sought God with tears and the final transformation occurred. God's heart finally beat within Jacob's own heart as he understood what was precious to God. This final trial shattered his flesh into submission as he realized all the wealth of flocks and herds can never replace the preciousness of a son. His inner man emerged and transformed the fleshly Jacob finally into a man God's presence could rest upon. He was now Israel, Prince of God. In doing so God would miraculously work all these terrible circumstances for Israel's and the family's good. Like the prodigal son who had labored within the pig pen, unknowingly, Israel was returning home to his father's house, where he would soon be draped in a royal robe and signet ring, insuring his identity with God as a worthy son was now complete.

> Trust in the Lord with all your heart and lean not to your own understanding. In all ways submit to Him and He will make your paths straight. Proverbs 3:5, 6. (NIV)

Jacob: Beauty for Ashes

One of the most powerful scenes in the movie *Shrek* is when the song "Hallelujah," by Leonard Cohen, is sung to reflect the brokenness of the main character Shrek when his love interest is about to marry another person. The song references some of the most notorious women of the Bible, including Bathsheba and Delilah. If we are honest with ourselves, none of us is a stranger to being broken. It is what we do on the other side of the event, to either choose bitterness and resentment or resolution and peace. We can choose to finish life's journey with grace and mercy towards our fellow and broken human beings.

The Japanese have turned brokenness into the art form Kintsugi. They take the broken pieces of china and instead of discarding them, they fill in the chipped or broken pieces with a gold paste. You might say that the piece has been given beauty for ashes. The result of the process is that the piece of china is adorned with gold and something once broken has been given a new life, adorned with beauty.

So it was with Jacob. Jacob's final recorded dream included him wrestling with God, seeing him face to face, and having his name changed from Jacob to Israel. By the end of his life Jacob (Israel) no longer used trickery to achieve his goals, but was humble, transparent and even reunited with his son Joseph in Egypt. We read that he blessed Pharaoh as he worshipped God on his staff in old age! Decades of shady dealings along with regrettable consequences had fashioned Jacob into maturity, nurtured by an intimate relationship with God. In his old age, the picture of Jacob is a beautiful one. God did what only He can do when someone has fully yielded their flesh and become "broken."

British evangelist Smith Wigglesworth said that each one of us has as much of the same Jacob nature in us. Our only hope is that the Lord may blaze away and destroy this outward flesh to such a degree, that the inner man will shine out and be seen. This is the only way for those of us who want to serve and lead others to the Lord. Famous Italian sculptor

Michelangelo said, "Every block of stone has a statue inside of it, and it is the task of the sculptor to discover it. I saw an angel in the marble and carved until I set him free." If we think of God as the sculptor and we are the blocks of stone. He must chip away the hard outside until the spiritual beauty within us has been given its freedom.

> "All else is limited in its value. Doctrine has some use as does theology. But what is the use of mere mental knowledge of the Bible if the outward man remains unbroken?" Smith Wigglesworth

We have seen from the life of Jacob that trials in our lives can actually help us to move forward into our God-given destiny if they are handled properly. Every Christian must be watchful, knowing that they must not only conquer their own flaws but become forbearing of the flaws of others. Maintaining an alert and prayerful posture will help us recognize our wily and destructive adversary. At times, he cloaks himself in human flesh that deceives us. We must become familiar with our spiritual armor and how to maximize its use in defeating the enemy.

> The weapons of our warfare are not carnal but mighty for pulling down strongholds. II Corinthians 10:4. (NKJV)

Many years ago, my mother gave me a beautiful antique cherry bureau that I thought was solid, cherry wood. One day, little chips of cherry veneer fell onto the rug. They revealed a much cheaper wood just beneath its surface. So it is with believers; we may possess the correct Christian lingo, sing songs, clap our hands and even say "praise the Lord" at appropriate intervals during the church service while the pastor is preaching. Is what we have solid or just a good looking veneer? When our lives encounter a "pothole in the road," do we find ourselves careening helplessly? Or are we able to lock arms with the brethren, dig deep into our spiritual roots, find our posture, and regain stride in our faith walk? If so, we can continue our journey, and defeat the foe of our soul.

The Second Garden: Gethsemane

God provided a way for us to have access as sons and daughters. Like the blood and skin of the animal that God supplied to provide a covering and sin offering for Adam and Eve. God's unfolding plan also included the shedding of blood, but this time it required a human sacrifice. The good news is that when we accept a relationship with *This Person,* who the scripture called the second Adam, the man and Savior, the Lord Jesus Christ, we now have access to the covering His blood provided.

> For just as through the disobedience of the one man the many were made sinners, so also through the obedience of the one man (Jesus) the many were made righteous. Romans 5:19. (NIV)

> When you were dead in your sins and in the uncircumcision of your flesh, God made you alive with Christ. He forgave us all our sins, having cancelled the charge of our legal indebtedness which stood against us and condemned; He has taken it away, nailing it to the cross. And having disarmed the powers and authorities, he made a public spectacle of them, triumphing over them by the cross. Colossians 2:13-15. (NIV)

In the second garden, called Gethsemane, Jesus was tempted by two choices. Fortunately, for us (and unlike Adam and Eve), He yielded Himself to what His Heavenly Father wanted. Jesus remembering the words of His Father and after being strengthened by prayer yielded His will to the will of God the Father. In obedience, He allowed himself to be crucified in the flesh on a cruel cross obediently as a sacrifice to pay the sin debt that Adam and Eve had incurred through disobedience. With confession and forgiveness, we now have access to eternity and the Tree of Life which was closed off when Adam and Eve sinned.

> And being found in appearance as a man, he (Jesus) humbled himself and became obedient unto death – even death on a cross. Philippians 2:8. (NIV)

> "Whoever eats my flesh and drinks my blood has eternal life, and I will raise them up on the last day." John 6: 54 (NIV)

The communion elements give us back what we lost in the Garden of Eden. That is access to the Tree of (Eternal) Life which is Jesus. When the adversary comes and challenges the promises that God has given to you, choose life, choose to believe what God says. Remember God, can never lie. Rely on Him to help you through any struggle and do not lean on your own wisdom and decide to become obedient unto death if necessary. The Holy Spirit's job is to conform us into the image of Christ, but to do so we may have to struggle through our issues and yield to God's will rather than our own.

> My little children, I am writing these things to you so that you may not sin. But if anyone does sin, we have an advocate with the Father, Jesus Christ the righteous. He is the expiation for our sins, and not for ours only but also for the sins of the whole world. I John 2: 1. (ESV)

In our Western churches, we only receive a little self-contained package with a wafer and a small portion of wine or grape juice. Next time you partake of communion, hold the elements and reflect on His beaten and bruised body and remember that by taking the cup and bread you are being restored back into a relationship with the Father and with each other. As believers, we should ask for forgiveness for any sin we have committed in our mind, by words or deed, against anyone plus any acts of omission, or for things that we should have done but neglected to do. This is called discerning the Lord's body. Scripture warns us that to not do this means we are actually bringing condemnation upon ourselves. Be reflective, humble and mindful of what communion with Christ is and do not take it unworthily or casually.

> Whoever therefore eats the bread and drinks the cup of the Lord in an unworthy manner will be guilty of profaning the body and blood of the Lord. Let a man examine himself, and so eat of the bread and drink of the cup. For anyone who eats and drinks without discerning the body eats and drinks judgment upon himself. This is why many of you are weak and ill, and some have died. I Cor. 11:27-30. (ESV)

> And he took the bread and gave thanks and broke it, and gave it to them (his disciples) saying, "This is my body given for you: do this in remembrance of me." In the same way after supper He took the cup after supper saying, "This cup is the new covenant in my blood, which is poured out for you." Luke 22: 19 - 20. (NIV)

If we have made a poor choice and headed in the wrong direction, it is comforting to know that a remedy has been provided. We must do our part by praying and seeking God for wisdom in the situation and then listen carefully for His instructions. If need be, repent and make a quality decision to turn around and intentionally head in the correct direction. Everyone makes poor choices from time to time. It is good to know that

God's mercy through the shed blood of His son provides forgiveness and wisdom for us always.

> Let us then approach God's throne of grace with confidence, so that we may receive mercy and find grace to help us in our time of need. Hebrews 4:16. (NIV)

> Therefore, since we have been justified by faith, we have peace with God through our Lord Jesus Christ Romans 5:1. (NIV)

Scriptures

1. Do not offer any part of yourself to sin, as instruments of wickedness, but rather offer yourselves to God, as those who have been brought from death to life; and offer every part of yourself to him as instruments of righteousness. For sin shall no longer be your master, because you are not under law but under grace. Romans 6:13 - 14 (NIV)

2. In all your ways submit to him and he will make your paths straight. Proverbs 3:6. (NIV)

Questions:

1. Jacob was a man "ruled by his flesh." Write about a trial that turned him from being a "broken man" to become a hero of faith.

2. What does it mean to be broken in the Biblical sense?

3. What did Jesus do that was different from Adam and Eve when He was confronted with a difficult choice?

4. How do the communion elements give us back what was lost in the Garden of Eden?

Action Goals

Have you identified a fleshly or 'stony' part of your life that has not yielded to God? It may have to do with your body, thought life, will or emotions. Prayerfully take the communion elements and ask for forgiveness and then submit this area to God. Does it help knowing that God can use any difficulty to conform you into the image of His Son Jesus? Read over the following declarations and choose one to confess daily over your specific situation. If this area seems too daunting to handle alone, then ask God to provide a person or group who can come into agreement and help you with accountability to get the victory in that area.

Scriptural Declarations:

Please note that some of the Scriptural Declarations are composites from Dr. Neil Anderson's book called *Helping Others Find Freedom in Christ.* They deal with how to bind demonic spirits that are keeping you from taking dominion in a specific area. They suggest to be free one must first verbally repent, renounce the lie and then choose to declare the truth over oneself. Realize it may take time to break old habits while forming new ones.

Declaration 1) Thank you Lord for purchasing me with the precious blood of Jesus, that He shed on the cross. I believe that Jesus died for my sins and that God raised Him from the dead and because of that I too will be raised up to newness of life. Scripture says if I confess with my mouth that Jesus is Lord and believe in my heart that God raised Him from the dead, I will be saved. (Rom. 10:9) I choose to live a holy life before you, Almighty God. I renounce all the works and ways of the enemy and any false input that has influenced my mind. I turn my back on my past sinful life and thank you for breaking any habits that keep me from releasing all the I am in Christ. God, please search my heart, go to the core of my being and cleanse me from any hidden sin and heal any hurts.

Declaration 2) I yield all of my fleshly members to you and commit to live a godly and holy life not relying on my will power but dependent on your Holy Spirit who graces and empowers me daily to live a pure and holy life. I yield myself and my members to God fully and completely, believing that the Holy Spirit's power is able to deliver me from any evil temptation daily. Whom the Son sets free, is free indeed. (Rom. 8:6). My mind is controlled by the Holy Spirit and my life is blessed and peaceful because I am a child of the Most High God. I am more than a conqueror through Him who loved me and am persuaded that nothing can separate me from the love of Christ. Neither death nor life, neither angels nor demons, neither anything in the present nor the future, nor any powers above or beneath, neither height nor depth, nor anything else will be able to separate me from the love of God which is in Christ Jesus my Lord.

Declaration 3) In the same way, I count myself dead to sin but alive to God in Christ Jesus. (Rom. 8:37-39) I will not let sin reign in my mortal body, nor will I obey its evil desires. I **do not** offer any part of my body, mind or emotions to be used as an instrument of wickedness, but rather yield myself to God and choose righteousness For sin shall not be my master, because I am not under the law but under grace (Rom. 6: 11-14). I choose to put off any thoughts or emotions that are inconsistent with who I am in Christ and what Christ did for me on the cross. I am saved, delivered, healed, whole and an overcomer who victoriously puts on Christ daily. I choose to be for you Lord totally and completely in my will, thoughts, and actions. Furthermore, if any voice in my head is contrary to what God's word has said that I am, then I will pull down those words and the voice of those words that tries to exalt itself against the knowledge of who God is in me and on that particular subject about me. Finally, I will not allow myself to be aligned with anyone who would try and influence me against what the will of God is for me. In the Name of Jesus, Amen.

Chapter Notes:

CHAPTER TEN

LEGACY

Jon Meachan wrote an observation from the life of Thomas Jefferson in his book the, *Art of Power*. "At the end of our days, all of us are going to be given a sentence of judgment according to the way we lived, by friends, family and the scriptures." This along with the observations and judgement of generations that follow will determine the legacy we leave." People are not the only ones who are going to judge our lives, God is.

> For God will bring every deed into judgment along with every secret thing, whether good or evil. Ecclesiastes 12:14. (NLT)

Continuing to read through the book of Genesis, we become better acquainted with Jacob's younger son, Joseph upon whose end, Jacob's legacy rested. From our last chapter we learned that Joseph's mother was the beautiful Rachel, Jacob's favorite wife. Having sons was important because it kept her influential in their household. Unfortunately Rachel met an untimely death bearing youngest son Benjamin. With her passing, all of Jacob's affection seemed to fall on son Joseph. Perhaps he reminded Jacob of his wife because the Bible picks up Joseph's life at seventeen and records that he was striking in form and appearance. He also demonstrated a refreshing contrast to his older brothers by developing an early sensitivity to the things of God and a talent for the family husbandry business. Trouble percolated because Joseph repeatedly gave evil reports to his dad about his older brothers' lackadaisical work ethic. They were further infuriated when Jacob showed favoritism to Joseph by rewarding him with a coat of many colors, an extravagant gift in those days. With this flamboyant display of affection and favor as Jacob's right hand man, it was only a matter of time before tensions began to flair. Joseph's close relationship with dad and his agreeable temperament positioned him as an obvious choice to take over the family business, and this did not sit well with the older brothers. What drove that final nail in the coffin was when Joseph began to have a series of dreams. They knew their father Jacob had been a dreamer and this seemed to confirm their worst nightmare. As the brothers contemplated a lifetime of the cocky heir's apparent leadership, a fanciful plan was hatched to ensure Joseph's demise.

Joseph's dreams were unusual. Although the family business was raising animals, Joseph's first dream involved sheaves of grains with his older brothers' sheaths bowing down to his. The next dream was about the heavens with the sun, moon and stars bowing down to him, which seem to symbolize that even his mother and father would bow in obedience to him. To the brothers this confirmed Joseph's arrogance. The household agreed that Joseph had gone too far with his grandiose dreams. Even Jacob rebuked his favorite son, saying, "Do you want even your mother and me to bow down to you?" As Joseph treasured all these things in his heart, he tried to work out what this meant and why the family was so stirred up. Wasn't it obvious that the family mantle and favor would bypass the older boys and land firmly on him? In the ancient Middle Eastern community, everyone knew that God communicated to his servants through dreams, so why didn't his family share Joseph's excitement about his favored future?

Mundane day, to day, events soon crowded out thoughts about what lay in the future. After the family's not so positive reaction, Joseph decided to put talk about his dreams aside so everyone's ruffled feathers would settle down. He never imagined that the festering hatred and resentment of his brothers would be daily rehearsed as they looked for more offenses. One day as Joseph approached them wearing his beautiful colored coat, with yet another batch of orders from Dad, the proverbial straw was broken. The brothers sprang into action as they saw an opportunity for revenge. Oldest brother Rueben was terrified at their plan and objected to the killing of Joseph and quickly looked for an alternative. The brothers fell upon Joseph, stripped him of his beautiful coat, (Genesis 37:23) and then threw him in a pit.

As Joseph languished in the pit, realizing his fate was sealed, he heard with horror for the first time the extent of their hatred towards him. Feasting triumphantly, they speculated upon the price Joseph would fetch from the slave traders. They never could have imagined the grief they were about to bring on Jacob and their household. Joseph was betrayed and sold for silver as a Christ like figure in the Old Testament. Consider this, that whenever anyone turns on their Christian brothers and sisters, they are repeating the crime of Joseph's brothers.

> So when the Midianites merchant came by, his brothers pulled Joseph out of the cistern and sold him for twenty shekels of silver to the Ismaelites who took him to Egypt. Genesis 37:28. (NIV)

A battered and humiliated Joseph was sold into slavery for twenty pieces of silver. Then he was auctioned off on a slave block to Potiphar, an Egyptian, who was also an officer and Captain of the Guard for Pharaoh. As time passed, Joseph's administrative talents surfaced and Potiphar noticed that with the handsome Israelite in charge, the entire household began to prosper because 'the Lord was with Joseph'.

And his master saw that the Lord was with him, and that the Lord made all that he (Joseph) did to prosper in his hand. Genesis 39:3. (KJV)

Then the testing season continued as Potiphar's wife took a fancy to Joseph and began to make advances toward him. Day after day, she tried to seduce him but because of Joseph's relationship with God, he refused her. Vexed and unhappy at the high moral ground of a house servant, she accused him of attempted rape. Again an innocent Joseph headed toward prison with no way out and *what about all his dreams?*

But he refused and said, "With me in charge," He told her, "The Master does not concern himself with anything, everything he owns he has entrusted to my care. No one in this house is greater than I am. My Master has withheld nothing from me except you because you are his wife. How could I do this great wickedness and sin against God?" And although she spoke to him day after day, he refused to go to bed with her or be with her. Genesis 39:8. (Berean)

Destiny Knocks

Even in prison, Joseph prospered, "because the Lord was with him." Again God's favor caught up with Joseph as he became head jailor in charge of the entire prison. One morning he noticed that the two new imprisoned officials from Pharaoh household looked pretty unhappy. One was official cupbearer to the king while the other was chief baker. When asked what was wrong, they replied that they had dreams they couldn't understand. Joseph replied, "Don't interpretations come from God? Tell me your dreams and I will interpret them." Joseph's prediction was that the cupbearer would be restored while the chief baker would be put to death. He was right about both dreams. As the cupbearer left prison Joseph said, "Remember me because I am innocent," but he quickly forgot about Joseph.

Not long after that Pharaoh had a dream that was so upsetting to him, he was unable to sleep, work or concentrate on anything else. To make matters worse, none of the advisors could explain the dream's meaning. Suddenly, the head cupbearer remembered Joseph. They had him cleaned up and presented to Pharaoh. Genesis 41 tells us about the dreams that Pharaoh had. He was standing by the Nile, and suddenly seven healthy cows come out of it and grazed on the marsh grass. They were followed by seven skinny cows. Next, Pharaoh dreamed that seven healthy ears of grain grew up out of a single stalk, but they were followed by seven thin and dried out ears. Like the cows, the thin stalks swallowed up the healthy ones. Joseph said, "The two dreams are one and the same. God is telling Pharaoh what He is about to do. Seven years of plenty are on their way and then there will be seven lean years. Put an experienced and wise administrator in charge of the country to store up food during the prosperous years for the years of famine that follow." You have to wonder if Joseph remembered his dreams of wheat long ago in Canaan.

After inquiring into Joseph's past and experience Pharaoh declared, "There doesn't seem to be anyone better qualified than you, Joseph, to oversee this enterprise, so the country won't be devastated by the famine. Only as king will I be over you." At thirty years of age and after thirteen years in captivity, in a micro-second Pharaoh had elevated Joseph to be his chief administrator and in charge of the entire country of Egypt. Pharaoh also took his royal signet ring of authority and put on Joseph's finger. Then Joseph was outfitted in the most splendid robes and a gold chain was placed around his neck. He was given the new name of Zaphenath-Paneah (God speaks and He lives) and to make his life complete, Asenath, the daughter of Potiphera, priest of On was given to him as a wife. Asenath gave him two sons, the first one was named Manasseh (Forget) and the second son was called Ephraim (Double Prosperity).

Joseph was well prepared for the administrative position and as he predicted there were seven years of prosperity. He wisely gathered the surplus and stockpiled as much grain and other food until there was no place to put it. Then the seven years of famine followed and the people went through all their surplus food. As the famine raged on, the people begged Joseph for food in exchange for their property. Food rations from the stockpile were given to them in exchange for their land and so because of Joseph, Pharaoh owned all the property of Egypt. Because of this world wide famine, soon other countries came knocking at Joseph's door. It was only a matter of time until Joseph's family in Canaan along with the brothers headed to Egypt.

Jacob learned there was food in Egypt, so he told his sons to go down and buy grain for the family. All of them were permitted to go except Benjamin, who Jacob kept back because he didn't want to lose him as he had lost Joseph. When the brothers arrived in Egypt, Joseph immediately recognized them. He began asking them questions about the family back home. They did not recognize him so they thought that this was unusual that he would be so curious about the family. Since they were at his mercy and needed supplies, they told him want he wanted to know and answered all of his questions.

> Then he remembered his dreams and said, "You are spies. You have come to see where our land is unprotected...and this is how you will be tested. As surely as Pharaoh lives, you will not leave this place until your youngest brother comes here. Send one of your number to get your brother; the rest of you will be kept in prison; so that your words may be tested to see if you are telling the truth." And he put them in custody for three days. Genesis 42:9, 15-17. (NIV)

On the third day Joseph said, "I am a God fearing man. If you are honest as you say, one of your brothers will stay in jail while the rest of you can take food back to your families." Simeon was kept back, while the rest had their sacks filled with grain and plenty of food for the journey home. Then Joseph returned all of their money back into their sacks. He also issued a stern warning saying they were not to return until they brought back the youngest brother. The brothers were so afraid that they began to argue among themselves saying they were being paid back for not being merciful to their brother Joseph when he cried out to them. The next day the brothers started back to Canaan leaving Simeon, but when they stopped for the night, they discovered all their money had been returned in their sacks. Puzzled at first, they soon realized the implications of this and became terrified.

Upon arriving home, they explained the predicament to father Jacob who was beside himself at loss of Simeon and the prospect of losing another son. He pleaded, "If you take Benjamin back and I lose him, I'll have nothing left." Reuben spoke up this time and tried to comfort his father with this promise, "If I don't return with Benjamin intact you can take my two sons and kill them. I promise with my life I will bring Benjamin back." Then Jacob asked why they had been so foolish to give the Egyptian so much personal information about their family saying they had another younger brother at home. They explained to Jacob that the man's questions had been so specific about their family including the youngest and their father. They could never have imagined the ultimatum he would give them. Without an alternative and with the food again dwindling, Jacob relented and sent Benjamin back with Reuben and his brothers to Egypt.

They brought back with them double their money, gifts and told the steward of Joseph's house about the mistake that had been made. Joseph's steward invited them in saying, "Everything is arranged, for your God and the God of your father must have given you a bonus." They were treated kindly and made to feel comfortable as they cleaned up. He explained they were going to have dinner with Joseph. Unable to work out why they were being singled in this way, they were fearful, wondering if the Egyptian was going to trick them, take them as slaves and keep the money and donkeys for himself. After all, that was what they would have done.

The high ranking administrator, Joseph, arrived home and greeted the brothers warmly, asking about their father and his health. He asked how the youngest brother was and then greeted Benjamin personally, "The Lord be gracious to you, my son." When Joseph saw Benjamin, he excused himself, left the room and burst into tears. After a time, he returned to the room and ate at his private table separate from the brothers. The brothers were seated in the order of their ages facing Joseph and their plates were piled high with food, but Benjamin was given a double portion. The brother's feasted and drank their full, leaving with their donkeys laden with all the food they could carry but in Benjamin's bag, Joseph hid his own special chalice. The brothers eager to return home, left early. Suddenly, they saw Joseph's steward and guards racing towards them. After searching through their belongings, they accused the brothers of stealing from their Master because they found the chalice that belonged to Joseph hidden in Benjamin's bag.

> "Why have you repaid evil for good? They assured him they didn't know what he was talking about but he insisted, "The Master's chalice has been stolen but the rest of you can go free, only the one who has the chalice on him will have to return with me to Egypt." Genesis 44:4, 7. (ESV)

Joseph was testing the brothers to see if they were still the same conniving brothers who only cared about themselves and would give up Benjamin easily to save their own skins. But instead the brothers wept, ripped their clothes and headed back to the city with the steward and Benjamin. When they arrived at the house each brother begged and pleaded with Joseph saying, "Please take me, as your slave, we cannot return without the lad or our poor old father will die." Then Joseph realized the brothers had indeed changed! Finally, Joseph couldn't take it anymore. He ordered all of his servants to leave the room and said, "Don't be afraid, I am Joseph." Then he wept and revealed himself to them. They were terrified and confused wondering what this could possibly mean.

> Then Joseph said to his brothers, "Come close to me." When they had done so, he said. "I am your brother Joseph, the one you sold into Egypt. And now, do not be distressed and do not be angry with yourselves for selling me here, because it was to save lives that God sent me ahead of you. Genesis 45:4-6. (NIV)

> But Joseph said to them, "Don't be afraid. Am I in the place of God? You intended to harm me, but God intended it for good to accomplish what is now being done, the saving of many lives. So then don't be afraid, I will provide for you and your children." Genesis 50: 19-21. (NIV)

Joseph explained that God knew that there was going to be a famine before it happened and had allowed these events to unfold so that Israel and the rest of his family would be preserved for posterity. He also explained to them that the famine was not over yet and there would be five more years of famine so they should go get their father and return to Egypt with their families so they would live. The brothers returned to Israel (Jacob) and told him that Joseph was now ruler of Egypt.

> So Israel (Jacob) set out with all that was his and when he reached Beersheba he offered sacrifices to God of his father Isaac. And God spoke to Israel in a vision in the night and said, "Jacob, Jacob! I am God, the God of your father."

He said, "Do not be afraid to go down to Egypt for I will make you into a great nation there. I will go down to Egypt with you, and I will surely bring you back again. And Joseph's own hand will close your eyes." As soon as Joseph appeared before Israel (in Goshen) he threw his arms around his father and wept for a long (long) time. Genesis 46:1-5, 29. (NIV)

Joseph's brothers and family grew to be a large clan. As promised Joseph did close the eyes of his father Jacob and was at his side when Jacob died as God had promised. Jacob and Joseph remind us that God has written a book that outlines all of the wonderful things that He has planned for us to do while we are here on earth. The prerequisite is simple. We must fully commit ourselves to the Lord and despite the difficulties continue to stay in relationship with God until His plans are realized.

Our Bible characters Jacob and Joseph give us a wonderful example of individuals who were flawed and yet decided to be obedient and allowed God to use them to effect the lives of many. As Jacob continued to yield himself fully to God, he produced a son who chose to forgive his brothers and didn't allow past events no matter how hurtful and wicked to interfere or shape his future life. Because of Joseph, his family, two nations and that region of the world were saved. If you are a believer being happy is not a sufficient goal because in this life you will have tribulation but be of good cheer because Jesus has overcome the world. You can too with God's help overcome any obstacle that comes your way knowing with God's help and strength you can fulfill His purpose and your destiny but the choice is yours to make.

Your eyes saw my unformed body, (and) all the days were written for me in your book before one of them came to be. Psalm 119:16. (Berean)

155

But the Pharisees and experts in the law rejected God's purpose for themselves, because they had not been baptized by John. Luke 7:30. (NIV)

Family Legacy

For as many years as I remember, my husband and our family have taken the long trek up the east coast from Florida to New England to the place where I grew up. Since my sister Darlene never left the area, a lot of family memorabilia has ended up at her house. This past year as Darlene was rifling through cardboard boxes of family treasures in her basement, she came upon something that she knew I would treasure. She handed me an old brown box to open and when I did, I lifted out a cherished heirloom. It was Grandma's enormous metal cooking spoon. I could hardly contain my excitement as my mind quickly slipped back to Grandma's kitchen where she created her famous and delicious Armenian delicacies. It was like receiving a baton from the previous generation indicating that it was my time to run. Examining the spoon, I reminisced upon those many delicious meals and pleasant memories.

My first memories of the large Victorian house on Hazel Park in Everett began with the summer of first grade, although according to family pictures I was taken there as a toddler. With school finally out for the summer holidays, mother carefully placed some of my clean clothes in a brown Star Market shopping bag, along with other necessary personal items including my favorite blue blanket. Then my mother and I were picked up by Uncle George in his old Chevy that always seemed to have a lingering hint of gasoline. As I carefully climbed into the back seat, my thighs would often stick to the hot plastic seats. Fortunately, on the way to Grandma's was a small Jewish bakery that had great prices for delicious day old Jewish pumpernickel bread and other yummy treats. The ancient grandmother behind the glass counter would wisely sway her large frame over to heavenly cinnamon rolls with frosting which inevitably caught my eye. It didn't take too much persuasion for my mom to include them in our purchase. Finally, we arrived at Grandma's house, and as Mom balanced all the bakery goods in her arms and opened the front screened door, an amazing waif of spices drifted out and beckoned us in. Mom would never dream of visiting without some groceries for the family. After washing my hands and face with Grandma's brown soap, I would also secure my hair neatly back with bobby pins. Then a homemade apron was placed over my outfit and I was allowed to sit up at the table and eat whatever yummy food was placed before me. It was usually Grandma's rice pilaf mounded up in an old pottery soup bowl.

Grandma stood just shy of 5 feet, but carried a commanding personality while speaking in her strange accent that included hand motions and a strange combination of English and Armenian. She sported a full head of frizzy white hair in a bun on top of her head, a couple of white tendrils always seemed to escape and fall on her wrinkled olive skinned cheek. Her outfit consisted of a type of patchwork homemade apron placed over a faded but clean flowered button up dress with oxford black lace up pump shoes completing her neat outfit. She always seemed to be stirring something in an enormous pot with her metal spoon while steam wafted towards the ceiling. I never understood why they were Uncle Georgie and Grandma because I thought they were husband and wife. To a little girl of six, they all looked about the same old age. Maybe it was explained and perhaps I wasn't paying attention but the next thing I knew, mom had gone, leaving me with this stranger who everyone just called Grandma.

Grandma's Sous Chef

I never realized how blessed I was to have such a wonderful family support system. Another year sped by with the end of the year routine upon me. No longer homesick, I eagerly anticipated summer because there was a safe and loving routine to look forward to where I was cared for, fed and able to play with many cousins and neighbors that lived nearby. As I got taller, I dashed easily up those six front stairs, flung open the screen and heavy front door and inhaled the welcoming and intoxicating aroma of spearmint, cumin, and allspice that awaited me in one of Grandma's tasty dishes. It was heavenly to experience a bowl of pilaf, fresh homemade yogurt, fried eggplant or salad paired with lemon and vinegar dressing or her incredible shells and tomato sauce. Sometimes, I would take a newly baked slice of Italian bread and push it into a bowl of her spaghetti sauce. My mouth is watering just thinking about it.

Having raised ten children of her own and now with the innumerable grandchildren, Grandma ran an orderly house with other family members and friends constantly dropping in. They would share their concerns as she listened carefully, handed out wisdom and sometimes the person shared the latest tidbit of neighborhood gossip. There was always plenty of laughter and no one ever left hungry. Family members and neighbors were always dropping off extra veggies or fruit from backyard gardens or farmer's markets. Sometimes they would share their favorite food or if we were really lucky some delicious Hood ice cream would miraculously appear from Uncle Humo and Aunt Yola's house. It seemed as though the endless list of family relatives stretched on forever with new little toddler cousins, being added yearly and brought systematically to Grandma's house where sudsy water, tub and clean towel waited. Children were bathed, given spotlessly clean clothes and then wrapped in a homemade quilted bib and placed in a chair at the table, so they could consume a bowl of Grandma's famous pilaf (rice) or chicken orzo soup served with her homemade mudzoom (yogurt).

There were always treasures to peruse through as bags of household items, clothing, shoes and other treasure were left in grocery bags in the front hallway by friends and family members. Our weekday daily routine was that after getting up, I got dressed, made my bed and fluffed my pillow and tidied myself and then brought down any laundry that needed cleaning. Uncle Bergie recently married, no longer needed his upstairs bedroom, so I slept in the old attic bedroom on the 3rd floor. I learned to hop down the two flights of stairs two or even three stairs at a time to a simple breakfast of tea with buttered pumpernickel toast or milk with bananas and cheerios. Grandma was always up before I was, working to keep everything spotlessly clean and in order.

Once a week when I came into the kitchen, she would be stirring a huge pot of bubbling bleached water on the stove with a wooden khashoon pot (paddle also used for corporal punishment) so her white sheets, towels and clothes would be meticulously cleaned. Afterwards, in the porcelain pantry sink tub, everything was rinsed, scrubbed again on a wash board with brown soap and carefully rinsed again and wrung out. The clean laundry would be hung on the clothesline to dry in the warm sun to finish its beauty treatment. Grandma had a method for everything and sometimes I would longingly look at the washing machine in the pantry, but Grandma felt it didn't clean the clothes properly. Fortunately there was something much more wonderful in it, chocolates. The wisdom of why this was done was too much for my small mind and I never questioned anyone about it because we weren't supposed to know they were in there.

My cousins and I would raid the chocolate box from time to time. Our secret seemed safe until one day the box of chocolates were served to Grandma's Armenian lady friends to accompany their afternoon tea. There was nothing in the box but empty wrappers and a few half bitten into candies. The shocked look on her face and then the warning murderous glance at us caused us grandchildren to scatter like rats off a sinking ship and we became quite scarce for a couple of hours. We blamed the half eaten candies on my Uncle Dickie, but truthfully my cousins and I had all participated in the crime.

With the afternoon came time to get the clothing off the line, we kids would stick our faces in the fresh sheets to inhale the intoxicating scent of fresh breezes and summer sun that seemed to be absorbed into every item of clothing. Many years after Grandma had passed away, we were getting rid of some of her sheets and pillow cases and you could still smell the wonderful outdoor fragrance on them. Preparation for the evening meal started in the morning right after the chores and house were put in order. I don't remember Grandma ever consulting a recipe; they all seemed to be neatly tucked in her brain under that tidy little bun. Obediently, I did what was asked, as her sous chef rolling tiny little meatballs for her meatball chicken soup that included chopped onions, spearmint or parsley which she expertly flavored with spices that she had dried herself. Perhaps that is where I picked up my love for cooking and organizing a household. Grandma always ordered five pounds of chicken necks and backs from Benny the meat man, which she cooked in a large pot of water on her stove. She separated the stock from the chicken pieces for her amazing rice pilaf, and then my job began. After the contents cooled sufficiently I separated tiny morsels of chicken from the bones, this was a job I loved because you got to snack on the meat and suck the marrow out of the bones. Sometimes, I had to head down the cellar for canned tomatoes or peaches. Or to mix things up, she would load up everything to fry the eggplant outside in the electric skillet on the porch. She didn't like her kitchen to have old food smells. With my chores done and lunch over, I bolted out the front door, free as a bird to head to the playground for the afternoon call on my cousins who lived nearby. One would think with such idyllic memories that Grandma had grown up in a nurturing home but that was not the case. She was an orphan raised in an orphanage in a war torn nation.

A Meaningful Life

Both sides of my family came from or more accurately I should say fled from the Western Armenian highlands also called Anatolia. My mother's family, the Mangerians traced their family home back to the village named Palu while my father's people traced back to a town called Kharpert (Harpoot). Both areas were located on the eastern leg of the Euphrates

River and had to endure the ravages of genocide prior to World War I under the ruthless Ottoman Empire. Despite the ravages and brutality of seeing parents, family members and friends butchered and beheaded, homes destroyed and villages burned, my Grandparents, Takouhy and John Mangerian, raised a family, established a loving home, cared for neighbors and their community while leaving their own grandchildren a rich legacy. As Orthodox Christians, they revered God, loved their family and cared for neighbors by being committed to forgiving past atrocities and did good while shunning evil. They refused to allow the bitterness of past events to undercut their present and future. They set a wonderful example for their children and grandchildren, and now I am blessed to pass this on to my own children and grandchildren.

My husband and I have seen firsthand how God is able to transform people right before our eyes if they partner with Him. What are you doing with your past? Are you allowing painful memories to keep you trapped in your past? Who or what is directing your life? Like Joseph and my Grandmother, someone is waiting at the end of your obedience if you are willing to keep moving forward and allow God to be in charge. There really aren't any other options for the true Christian.

Scriptures

1. So then each (one) of us will give an account of ourselves to God. Romans 14:12. (NIV)

2. But as for you, what you meant for evil against me, but God meant it for good. Genesis 50:20. (NKJV)

3. The Father judges no one but has given all judgement to the Son, that all may honor the Son just as they honor the Father. Do not marvel at this, that an hour is coming when all who are in the tombs will hear his voice and come out, those who have done well

to the resurrection of life, and those who have done evil to the resurrection of judgement. John 5:21-31. (ESV)

Questions:

1. How can a quality decision change the direction of your life?

2. What role did interpreting the dreams of the baker and cupbearer play in helping Joseph appear before Pharaoh?

3. How did interpreting Pharaoh's dream help Joseph to fulfill his destiny?

4. What are the two thrones mentioned in Revelation and what role do they play in destiny?

5. What were the positive attributes or legacy that the author received for her grandparents?

Action Plan

Think about and write down what kind of legacy that you would like to leave behind for others?

Prayerful/Confessions:

Heavenly Father thank you for all that I have learned from this chapter. I make the decision to forgive any person who has sinned against me and make a quality decision with God's help to keep my appointment with destiny like Joseph did. I will make the decision to continue to use the gifts and talents that You have blessed me with and will not allow the pain of my past to keep me from venturing out and pursuing my future. Thank you for blessing and assisting me as I lean on the guidance and wisdom of

Holy Spirit to get me through the refining process. Grant me grace in spite of life's difficulties that I might participate in your training to continue until completion that I might be fully prepared for the tasks ahead. I will ask, seek and knock at God's door with tenacity, courage and be fierce but humble in pursuing all that you have for me. I will not act prematurely but will wait until you open the door of opportunity. I will not allow myself to birth Ismael, but will wait for Isaac. May I be used to help others succeed and help to me to never to be an obstacle or hindrance in any person's life. I will involve myself with the lives of the individuals in my sphere of influence that they too may be blessed and because of me, they will fulfill their God given destiny through Jesus Christ our Lord. Amen

Chapter Notes

BIBLIOGRAPHY AND RESOURCES THAT THE AUTHOR FOUND HELPFUL

Books

Anderson, Neil T. *The Bondage Breaker*. Eugene: Harvest House: 2000.

Austin, Eileen. *Out of the Belly of the Whale*. Bloomington: iUniverse: 2009.

Beattie, Melody. *Codependents Guide to the Twelve Steps*. Parkside: Simon and Schuster: 1992.

Bevere, John. *The Holy Spirit*. Palmer Lake: Messenger International: 2013.

Bogosian, Eric. *Operation Nemesis*. New York: Little Brown and Co.: 2015.

Bonke, Reinhart. *Holy Spirit: Are You Flammable or Fireproof?* Orlando: Christ for All Nations: 2017.

Brown, Carol A. *Highly Sensitive Emotions*. Shippensburg: Destiny Image: 2010.

Cloud, Dr. Henry and Dr. John Townsend. *Boundaries: When to Say Yes, How to Say No to Take Control of Your Life*. Grand Rapids: Zondervan: 1996.

Dumas, Alexander. *The Count of Monte Cristo*. New York: Baronet Books: 1992.

Dungy, Tony. *Quiet Strength.* Wheaton: Tyndale House: 2007.

Edwards, Gene. *Tale of Three Kings.* Newnan: Seed Sowers: 1980.

Frangipane, Francis. *The Three Battlegrounds.* Cedar Rapids: Arrow Publications: 2002.

Goll, Jim. *The Seer.* Shippensburg: Destiny Image: 2004.

Kenyon E. W. *The Blood Covenant.* Kenyon Gospel Publishing Society: 1969.

LaHaye, Tim. *Spirit Controlled Temperament.* Wheaton: Tyndale House: 1981.

Nee, Watchman. *Spiritual Authority.* New York: Christian Fellowship: 1972.

Nee. Watchman. *The Spiritual Man.* New York: Christian Fellowship: 1968.

Prince, Derek. *The Foundation Series.* Ft. Lauderdale: Derek Prince Publishing: 1966.

Sazzero, Peter. *Emotional Healthy Spirituality.* Nashville: Thomas Nelson: 2006.

Seamands, David. *Healing for Damaged Emotions.* Colorado Springs: David C. Cook: 1981.

Article

"My Trainwreck Conversion", *Christianity Today Magazine,* Dr. Rosarrio Butterfield.

Websites

bjm.org....Bill Johnson Ministries

ChristineCaine.com....Christian Caine Ministries

Lifestylechristianity.com.....Todd White Ministries

https://sidroth.org It's Supernatural with Sid Roth

www.joycemeyer.org.....Joyce Meyer Ministries

thehotline.org....1 800 799 7233 National Domestic Violence

www.suicidewatch 1800 273 8255 National Suicide Prevention Lifeline

Movies

Amazing Grace (2006) - William Wilberforce and the heroic campaign to end slavery.

Chariots of Fire (1981) - Eric Liddell, Gold Medal winner in the 400 meter race in the 1924 Olympic Games in Paris.

Printed in the United States
by Baker & Taylor Publisher Services